Why do People Suffer?

Why do People Suffer?

JAMES JONES

LION

A Lion Book
an imprint of
Lion Hudson plc
Mayfield House, 256 Banbury Road,
Oxford OX2 7DH, England
www.lionhudson.com
ISBN 978 0 7459 5238 3

First edition 1993
Second edition 2007
10 9 8 7 6 5 4 3 2 1 0

Acknowledgments

p. 38 Scripture quotation is taken from the New Revised Standard Version
published by HarperCollins Publishers, copyright © 1989 by the Division
of Christian Education of the National Council of the Churches of Christ
in the USA, and is used by permission. All rights reserved.

All other scripture quotations are taken from the Holy Bible, New
International Version, copyright © 1973, 1978, 1984 International
Bible Society. Used by permission of Zondervan and Hodder & Stoughton
Limited. All rights reserved. The 'NIV' and 'New International Version'
trademarks are registered in the United States Patent and Trademark Office
by International Bible Society. Use of either trademark requires the permission
of International Bible Society. UK trademark number 1448790.

Other quotations are taken from the following sources:

p. 8 M. Scott Peck, *The Road Less Travelled*, Simon & Schuster, 1978.

p. 13 James Joyce, *A Portrait of the Artist as a Young Man*, Penguin, 1992.

pp. 13, 55 Nicholas Wolterstorff, *Lament for a Son*, Hodder & Stoughton, 1987.

p. 22 Richard Holloway, *Paradoxes of Christian Faith and Life*, Mowbrays, 1984.

pp. 70–71 Clifford Longley, 'Why doesn't a good God intervene to prevent evil?',
The Times, London, 28.12.91.

p. 108 C. S. Lewis, *The Problem of Pain*, Fount, 1977.

p. 110 Julian of Norwich, quoted by Grace Jantzen in *Julian of Norwich, Mystic
and Theologian,* SPCK, 1987.

A catalogue record for this book is available
from the British Library

Typeset in 12/14 Lapidiary333 BT
Printed and bound in China

Contents

CHAPTER ONE

Life is difficult

It is remarkable that in a world of such dreadful suffering so many people should persist in believing in a good and loving God. It is in spite of the evil, and not because of it, that people hold on to such a faith. The fact of suffering is the strongest and the loudest argument against there being a God at all.

The loneliness of suffering

The twenty-first century has barely begun but already its pages are written in tragedy. The day after Christmas 2004 nearly

Rescue workers at Ground Zero search the wreckage of the twin towers of the World Trade Center, New York, following the attacks of 9/11.

half a million people were swept away by the Asian tsunami. Two days later – Holy Innocents Day, which commemorates the slaughter of children by King Herod – the world was counting the cost of innocent lives destroyed by one of the greatest natural disasters in history. All over the world people grieved for the loss of those they loved. Video images brought the full horror into the homes of many as surely as the waves that swept through the chalets, the hotels, the huts and the villages. The destruction showed no favours and respected no persons as rich and poor alike drowned in the tidal surge that sucked the life from the beaches into the deep.

Although the scale of the devastation caused by the tsunami was new, the human family has never been a stranger to natural calamities. But this disaster had come only three years after nineteen fanatical terrorists visited carnage on the World Trade Center in New York and the Pentagon in Washington. These symbols of the commercial

The question, 'How can you believe in a God who permits suffering on this scale?' is therefore very much around at the moment, and it would be surprising if it weren't – indeed it would be wrong if it weren't.

Rowan Williams [after the 2004 Asian tsunami]

and military might of America were crushed by suicidal warriors who showed that a civilization could be subjected to hitherto unimaginable terror. Here were human beings bent on human suffering, inflicting terrifying mortal wounds on themselves and their enemies. Such is the capacity of the human race for self-destruction that it has prompted Sir Martin Rees, the Astronomer Royal, to wonder aloud whether we have more than a 50/50 chance of surviving the twenty-first century. In spite – or because – of our technological and scientific advances we now have the ability to afflict ourselves with new degrees of physical and mental suffering.

The difficulties of life

Life is difficult. This is a great truth, one of the greatest truths… Most do not fully see this truth that life is difficult. Instead they moan more or less incessantly, noisily or subtly, about the enormity of their problems, their burdens, and their difficulties as if life were generally easy, as if life should be easy… I know about this moaning because I have done my share. Life is a series of problems.

M. SCOTT PECK

Most of us go through life constantly surprised when something hard or painful happens to us. We seem to expect that life should be a smooth path. That's certainly the view of the majority of people who live in the 'first world'. There have been such advances in medical science that somehow we feel cheated if the doctors can't find a cure for our diseases. Many people have good access to excellent health care, and consequently live much longer. But this has encouraged an attitude in these privileged circles that pain and suffering are unnatural intrusions into life. Death itself, far from being seen as part of a natural cycle, is spoken of in hushed tones. It's some secret enemy that has taken someone by surprise. Yet dying is as frequent a human experience as being born.

Suffering is in the fabric of our lives. There is no life without pain – be it mental, physical, emotional or spiritual. That's the way we are. That's the nature of things. We can go through life either constantly taken aback by every difficulty that troubles us, or ready and braced to face the problems that will inevitably come our way. The former attitude is less likely to equip us for life. The latter outlook, although more realistic and healthier, still leaves us asking questions about why there should be suffering in the first

An Acehnese woman at the ruins of her home in downtown Banda Aceh, a month after a powerful tsunami hit the region on December 26 2004, following a submarine earthquake which left 228,429 people dead or missing.

place, and how a God of love can allow a world of suffering to exist.

> For sufferance is the badge of all our tribe.
>
> *William Shakespeare*

There's a loneliness in suffering. It always feels as if we are the only person in the world to suffer in this way. It feels as if everybody else is all right. Their world seems to hold together. It is only ours that is falling apart. Life goes on for everybody else. Ours alone has stopped. We look around through our tears. People carry on doing the things they do unaware and unaffected by the calamity that has devastated us. If only they knew.

Yet, even if they did, life would still go on. People would carry on eating and opening windows and going to work. The world doesn't stop just because we suffer. That's how it feels and that's why we feel so isolated when we suffer. Marooned and friendless on an island wilderness. And even when people visit us and try to comfort us we know that

The cry of Job

*Even today my complaint is bitter;
[God's] hand is heavy in spite of my
groaning. If only I knew where to
find him; if only I could go to his
dwelling! I would state my case
before him and fill my mouth with
arguments. I would find out what
he would answer me, and consider
what he would say... But if I go to
the east, he is not there; if I go to
the west, I do not find him. When
he is at work in the north, I do not
see him; when he turns to the
south, I catch no glimpse of him.
But he knows the way that I take;
when he has tested me, I shall
come forth as gold.*

JOB 23:2–5, 8–10

soon they will leave us and return to their routine. They will
abandon us to our solitude and to the suffering that no one
else can ever enter into and share with us.

The darkness of the suffering is made more dense by the
sense that there will be no end to the pain. When people try
to comfort us with 'you'll soon be all right,' we have neither
the energy nor the inner resources to cope with their
reaction should we, to their faces, call them liars. We feel
that they are false comforters. We say nothing, smile limply
and resign our souls to the long night that has no morning.
The darkness of suffering envelops us and obscures all rays
of hope. That is its very nature. It feels like a life sentence.

Inevitably we hear a chorus of one shouting in our heads
'Why me?' It is not so much an intellectual question asking
for reasons as a cry of a soul looking for attention. Although
we doubt that anybody can fully share our sadness there is

> Suffering is
> permanent,
> obscure and
> dark,
> and shares
> the nature of
> infinity.
>
> *William
> Wordsworth*

still an inner urge to find someone who will, like a parent, devote themselves to us and somehow make it better. But that person must know what it's like to suffer in the way that we are suffering; they must be as concerned for us as they are for themselves. Such compassionate friends are few and far between.

The absence of such comforters who will show us genuine pity leaves us settling for the one person who does suffer as much as we do and who is equally concerned for our own welfare – our self. Here is the beginning of self-pity. Self becomes the preoccupation of our own attention. We lick our wounds. In the chamber of our soul we echo the tearful song of self-pity, 'Why me?'

It is often in the mire of self-pity, when we have tired for a while of feeling sorry for ourselves, that we raise our eyes and look around and above. Before we have time for the intellectual arguments to form in our minds we find words forming a prayer, 'Why me, God?' The cry is just the same as before, but the arena has changed. Instead of a world dominated by our own situation, we have pushed out the boundaries and included the possibility of God.

I say the possibility of God deliberately because most people – indeed, all people – who start praying do so very tentatively. The first prayers of 'infant' adults are cautious and full of hesitation. They are no less real and no less valuable because of that. They are often angry, 'I thought you were meant to be a God of love!'; sometimes questioning, 'How could you let such a thing happen?'; sometimes seeking, 'But why?'; sometimes bitter and resentful, 'Well if that's how you treat people...'; sometimes bargaining, 'If you do this and... then I will promise to...'

Yet these prayers, however they are uttered, represent a transformation in our perceptions. We have begun to imagine a world in which there is now possibly not just one but two principal characters, self and God. As that perception enlarges, the intellectual arguments often begin to marshall themselves for and against the possibility of God. And just as suffering brings us to the threshold of wondering

> Pity is the feeling which arrests the mind in the presence of whatsoever is grave and constant in human sufferings and unites it with the human sufferer.
>
> *James Joyce*

The face of God

It is said of God that no one can behold his face and live. I always thought this meant that no one could see his splendour and live. A friend said perhaps it meant that no one could see his sorrow and live. Or perhaps his sorrow is his splendour.

NICHOLAS WOLTERSTORFF

if there is a God, it is suffering which itself presents the fortified wall against entering in and believing. Like a piston, suffering both pushes us upward and pulls us back with equal force.

We go in search of a God who has all the answers, who will make sense of the apparently senseless, who will perhaps give back what has been lost, who might heal the disease, who will make good what is bad. We reach out to God to help us, desperate to transform our sadness into peace.

But even as we reach out, suffering is ready to pull us away from all that we are aspiring to find. We fall back under the pressure of all the unanswerable questions. Why does a God of love allow such evil in the world? Did God make the evil? What sort of God would create a world of pain and suffering? Can there really be an all-powerful and loving God at all? Perhaps the world's been made by an evil force? Maybe God has no interest in us, leaving us just to get on with it, so there's no point in praying?

It is these questions more than any others that make a belief in God so difficult for many people, and not just for those who are suffering at the time. There is not one person who does not at some stage in life pray. Whenever prayers start rising within the soul these questions arise in the mind. Suffering is the greatest obstacle to faith in God. Yet it is also the greatest incentive.

As we reflect on suffering in the world there are two ways of proceeding. We can build on the premise that there is no God and that suffering is simply a fact of human existence — its only significance is that men and women are born to suffer. The value of suffering is measured only by the virtues that it draws out of humanity, such as courage, nobility, patience, sacrifice. But without God there is no overall purpose and meaning to life and its inevitable fabric of suffering. Suffering is simply a fact of life. It gives the atheist no difficulty.

Suffering becomes a problem only when one starts

exploring the alternative view that this world of sorrow and pain has been fashioned by a good and loving God. It is that problem that this book sets out to explore. Through the centuries and across the world, faith in God has given people who suffer some meaning to their existence, and sustained them even in the most appalling abyss of human suffering.

The fact of suffering

Everybody suffers. Not everyone suffers to the same degree or in the same way. But there is nobody on the face of the earth who is a stranger to suffering. There's the suffering of someone dying of cancer, every part of the personality being affected:

● the mental fear of the process of dying

● the emotional turmoil of leaving those you love

● the physical pain of a body wasting away

● the spiritual distress of not knowing what lies beyond

● the personal loneliness of going down the path alone.

Although we don't all die of cancer, all of us experience to some degree some aspects of suffering.

Mental suffering

Mental fears cause a great deal of suffering. Even imaginary fears are real fears to the person who's frightened. People who are afraid of walking out into open spaces may not even know what they're frightened of. Rationally they may be able to see that there is nothing that will physically harm them. But that doesn't stop them being overwhelmed by an irrational fear that fills them with dread and paralyzes them. Their suffering is real.

Emotional suffering

Emotional turmoil swirls around us throughout our lives. Sometimes it's a gentle breeze, other times it can cause havoc like a destructive tornado. Emotional suffering is universal; we all know what it is to feel intense swings of mood. These can be brought on either by circumstance or by chemical changes in our bodies. Feeling low can go hand in hand with a loss of perspective that robs you of the confidence that things will ever change, let alone get better. It is the combination of a depressed mood and a lack of hope that makes it difficult to cope with life and causes so much emotional suffering. Such episodes are aggravated by long-term situations that seem impossible to change.

Debt, stress, work–life balance and poor relationships

War veterans hold their Armistice Day Parade on the eleventh hour of the eleventh day of the eleventh month at Bedworth Cenotaph on 11 November 2005 in Bedworth, England.

can add pressure to the emotional cauldron. They can even lead to drug dependency and addiction, especially where there is a history of low self-esteem or self-hatred.

Someone very close to us dies suddenly. At first we refuse to believe it. Then when the news has sunk in we get angry, rooting out someone to blame – the doctors, God, ourselves. The anger gives way to self-pity and we wonder how we shall cope and who will take the irreplaceable place of the one who's gone. Then a dark cloud envelops us. Inside there's a bitter flatness like a stale bottle of tonic water. We enjoy nothing. The things that entertained us – our favourite meal, programme, hobby, holiday, friendship – leave us unfulfilled and disappointed. There are no comforters. Those who do not speak of the one we've lost make us feel rejected, dejected and depressed. Those who tell us that it's time we built a new life fill us with despair. The suffering is very real.

Physical suffering

Physical pain afflicts us all at some stage. And in some situations it's just as well that we do feel pain. Although it is tragic that a small child burns herself and screams when she goes too near a fire, at least the pain makes her recoil and stops her being killed. Pain is a warning signal of impending danger.

But whereas we can see the benefit of the short, sharp shock of pain to alert us to a hidden danger, what is more difficult for us to bear is the sustained period of pain which in some cases is unremitting – a slipped disc, osteoarthritis, incessant migraines. This sort of pain is hard to endure. Friends and family may be initially sympathetic, but soon they tire of hearing of our troubles. The effect is debilitating. It saps our energy.

Spiritual suffering

Over and above the suffering that afflicts the mind, the emotions and the body, there's a spiritual disease which we all suffer from. It's to do with the part of our personality that aspires to find some meaning for our existence. What are we here for? Where did we come from? Where are we bound for? What, if anything, lies beyond this existence? Although few of us think about these questions all the time, there isn't a person who doesn't at some stage in his or her life start prodding at them and wondering if there are any answers to be found.

It is very often at a time of crisis that we begin to search seriously for some answers. When the bottom falls out of our life, when we come close to death, these are moments when we look at ourselves and what we have achieved and become aware of our own insignificance. Our lives begin to look like footprints in the sand that will soon be erased as the next wave of time rolls on and washes over the place where we have been. This sense of insignificance and meaninglessness is the source of a spiritual suffering that drives us to look for medicine of a spiritual kind. Yet while we wait for the remedy, the spiritual suffering can become very intense. It's these and other experiences of suffering that have inspired artists, composers, poets and novelists.

If a bird is flying for pleasure it flies with the wind, but if it meets danger it turns and faces the wind in order that it may rise higher.

Corrie Ten Boom

CHAPTER TWO

Where did suffering come from?

If God, who made the world, is good, how did he ever allow suffering to invade the universe? And if God is responsible for all that exists, is he also responsible for all the suffering that we see? But if this suffering is not from God, then where has it come from?

Conflict with God in the spiritual world

In the last book of the Bible, Revelation, there is a picture of heaven. It is a kaleidoscope of images of the spiritual realm. This world is not accessible to human eyes. Neither

God nor his angels can be seen – as spiritual beings they are beyond the physical world and its limitations. They are real, but they are not bound by the constraints of time and space.

We can gain access to the world of the spirit that lies beyond the material world only through images and pictures. They do not tell us the whole story. They do not give us all the dimensions of the spiritual reality.

Just as a photograph fails to give you all the dimensions and the full reality of a situation, so images in the book of Revelation and in other parts of the Bible do not give us the whole story. Nevertheless, in Revelation, there are occasional pictures that explore the relationship between good and evil and, in particular, zoom in on the main conflict between God and his enemies.

The limits of human understanding

A photograph of a three-dimensional object only ever has two dimensions. The viewer can see only the image, not the whole

situation. It is limited in that it does not allow the viewer to feel, to smell, to taste, to hear that which has been photographed. In the same way, eternal truths about God are passed to human minds through picture language such as that in the book of Revelation. What they are able to convey is limited. Through them we see only a part of the truth. Paul, the apostle, wrote about this in his first letter to the

The mystery of faith and suffering

Suffering may be a problem for the believer, but it is a problem that arises as a result of faith and it cannot logically be used as an argument against it.

A clumsy analogy from medicine might illustrate this. Let us suppose that I contract a deadly disease that will kill me unless it is checked and controlled by suitable treatment. The doctors put me onto a drug called X, which controls the disease and assures me of a normal life span. Unfortunately, the drug has certain unpleasant and unavoidable side effects which the doctors do not yet entirely understand, though they are constantly struggling with the problem. The drug impairs my eyesight and gives me periodic headaches. This life-giving medicine brings with it certain painful and unalterable disadvantages.

I can do either of two things: I can continue to take the drug and cope with the problems though I do not like or understand them. Or I can rail wildly against the drug and its manufacturers and their good faith in marketing it in the first place. I can give up the use of the drug.

My vision improves and my headaches disappear, and in a few years I am dead.

We live in a mysterious universe. Belief in a good God lights up that mystery and gives it meaning. The fundamental problem of life's meaning is resolved by faith. But faith, in turn, gives rise to certain derivative problems, such as the problem of suffering. To give up faith because of the problems that derive from it is as foolish as giving up a life-giving medicine because of its unpleasant side effects. In each case the avoidance of the problem only leads to death.

The person who gives up belief in God because it brings with it certain unresolvable dilemmas ends up by believing in a dying universe in which there is no meaning anywhere, a universe that came from nothing and goes to nothing, a universe that is cruelly indifferent to all our needs.

And there is no point in feeling resentment against such a universe, because in a godless universe there is no reason why anything should not happen, and there is no one to resent, no one to blame.

RICHARD HOLLOWAY

Corinthians: 'Now we see but a poor reflection, as in a mirror; then we shall see face to face. Now I know in part; then I shall know fully, even as I am fully known' (1 Corinthians 13:12).

It is important to understand what these pictures meant when they were first seen, and not to try to interpret them according to our own ideas.

One of the most vivid images in Revelation is of a battle in heaven. The cause of the conflict is not given. But there are clues in the names of people (a common theme in the ancient world). The enemy of God is named here and elsewhere in the Bible as the devil or Satan. Devil means 'the one who throws things at another'. (In Greek, the language of the New Testament, it is *diabolos* from which we get the word diabolical.) Satan means 'accuser', someone who attacks the integrity of another. Both words suggest that this enemy of God had a freedom and an independence to challenge God even though God made him.

Read the short section of this story, *A war against God*. Bear in mind that this is a visionary image that does not tell us the whole story. But there are details that help our understanding of the relationship between evil and good.

A war against God

And there was war in heaven... The great dragon was hurled down – that ancient serpent called the devil, or Satan, who leads the whole world astray. He was hurled to the earth, and his angels with him.

Then I heard a loud voice in heaven say: 'Now have come the salvation and the power and the kingdom of our God, and the authority of his Christ. For the accuser of our brothers, who accuses them before our God day and night, has been hurled down... woe to the earth and the sea, because the devil has gone down to you! He is filled with fury, because he knows that his time is short.'

REVELATION 12:7, 9–13

Spiritual beings such as Satan possess a freedom similar to that of human beings

They have a choice to stand for or against God. Satan exercises his freedom to challenge God. (In a later chapter we explore the reason why God gives his creatures such freedom.)

The power of the devil is inferior to that of God

He is defeated in the struggle. Although the devil continues to be active, he is not as powerful as the forces of God. In other words, we do not live in a universe where the forces of good and evil are evenly matched.

The rebellion of the devil and his angels leads to their expulsion from heaven

Angels Fighting by Gustave Dore, illustration to Milton's Paradise Lost.

God will not compromise with evil. He gets rid of this evil from heaven as a first step to removing all its destructive traces from his creation.

Although thrown out of heaven, the devil is not destroyed

He is active outside heaven in the world of human affairs. Like a poisonous yet odourless gas the devil pervades the universe, and exercises an influence that drives the human family away from God.

His time is short

Every day on television we see crimes and catastrophes which cause human suffering. The book of Revelation suggests powerfully that these days will end – the image is of the evil one being thrown off the earth and destroyed.

In Rwanda we saw children and women butchered as extremist Hutus led a savage, merciless slaughter of Tutsis and moderate Hutus. Hundreds of thousands were eliminated not by natural disasters but by the whim of human nature in the grip of evil. It felt as if some great cosmic and spiritual battle between good and evil was

> **It is stupid of modern civilization to have given up believing in the devil, when he is the only explanation of it.**
>
> *Ronald Knox*

25

How it all began

God makes the world
In the beginning God created the heavens and the earth. Now the earth was formless and empty, darkness was over the surface of the deep, and the Spirit of God was hovering over the waters.

And God said, 'Let there be light,' and there was light. God saw that the light was good, and he separated the light from the darkness. God called the light 'day' and the darkness he called 'night'. And there was evening, and there was morning – the first day.

God makes people in his own image
And God said, 'Let the land produce living creatures according to their kinds: livestock, creatures that move along the ground, and wild animals, each according to its kind.' And it was so. God made all the creatures that move along the ground according to their kinds. And God saw that it was good.

Then God said, 'Let us make man in our image, in our likeness, and let them rule over the fish of the sea and the birds of the air, over the livestock, over all the earth, and over all the creatures that move along the ground.'

So God created man in his own image,
in the image of God he created him;
male and female he created them.

God blessed them and said to them, 'Be fruitful and increase in number – fill the earth and subdue it. Rule over the fish of the sea and the birds of the air and over every living creature that moves on the ground.'

God saw all that he had made, and it was very good. And there was evening, and there was morning – the sixth day.

So the man gave names to all the livestock, the birds of the air and all the beasts of the field. But for Adam no suitable helper was found. So the Lord God caused the man to fall into a deep sleep; and while he was sleeping, he took one of the man's ribs and closed up the place with flesh. Then the Lord God made a woman from the rib he had taken out of the man, and he brought her to the man.

The man said, 'This is now bone of my bones and flesh of my flesh; she shall be called "woman", for she was taken out of man.' For this reason a man will leave his father and mother and be united to his wife, and they will become one flesh. The man and his wife were both naked, and they felt no shame.

Challenge to God
Now the serpent was more crafty than any of the wild animals the Lord God had made. He said to the woman, 'Did God really say, "You must not eat from any tree in the garden"?'

The woman said to the serpent, 'We may eat fruit from the trees in the garden, but God did say, "You must not eat fruit from the tree that is in the middle of the garden, and you must not touch it, or you will die."'

'You will not surely die,' the serpent said to the woman. 'For God knows that when you eat of it your eyes will be opened, and you will be like God, knowing good and evil.'

When the woman saw that the fruit of the tree was good for food and pleasing to the eye, and also desirable for gaining wisdom, she took some and ate it. She also gave some to her husband, who was with her, and he ate it. Then the eyes of both of them were opened, and they realized that they were naked; so they sewed fig leaves together and made coverings for themselves.

Then the man and his wife heard the sound of the Lord God as he was walking in the garden in the cool of the day, and they hid from the Lord God among the trees of the garden. But the Lord God called to the man, 'Where are you?' He answered, 'I heard you in the garden, and I was afraid because I was naked; so I hid.'

EXTRACTS FROM GENESIS 1–3

God confronts Adam and Eve in the Garden of Eden following their disobedience. Stained glass from Malvern Priory, Worcestershire.

being played out on earth as the devil darkened the imagination of human beings, making eyes blind and ears deaf to the plight of innocence.

The conflict with God in the spiritual world directly leads to a conflict with God in the material world on earth. Jesus himself encountered the antagonism of the devil. He identified him as 'the father of lies' who deceives people and as 'the prince of this world' who influences people, targeting those in leadership, enticing them away from God. The evil one is real.

Conflict with God in the material world

Jesus said, 'I saw Satan fall like lightning from heaven' (Luke 10:18). This image speaks of the powerfully destructive force of evil in the world. It suggests, as does the vision in Revelation, that the evil disorder which produces so much pain and misery in the world has its origins in a reality over and above and beyond the material world.

But how exactly does spiritual evil affect the physical world? Again, all that we have are biblical images that offer clues. They do not tell us the whole story, neither do they answer every question. Turning from the last book in the Bible to the first book, Genesis, we find a story that describes a basic connection between the spiritual world opposed to God and the physical world of human beings.

There are different views of how literally this story is meant, but certainly it teaches us about God's relationship to his creation. We must be careful not to overstate an interpretation of these stories, but there are points that ought to be highlighted as we explore the connection between good and evil.

The physical world exists because of the spiritual world

Right at the start the material world was brought into being by God, who is spirit. There is a spiritual connection between creator and creation.

The material world is originally good

Whatever state it is in now does not contradict the view that the original act of creation by God was essentially good.

When it came to creating the human family God acted in a different and unique way

In all the other acts of creation, God said 'Let there be...' It's an almost impersonal statement. But when it came to making man and woman God said, 'Let us make them in our image...' Here was an intimately personal act of creation. Although it is not clear what the phrase 'image of God' means, the way it is used here and in other parts of the Bible speaks of our value in the eyes of God, and of a special relationship between God and humanity. Even though God is spirit and we are flesh and blood, there is a spiritual dimension to our own lives so that we can know and connect with God on a spiritual level.

God delegates responsibility for the rest of creation to human beings

This image is very relevant to life in the twenty-first century. We have recently become awesomely aware of our responsibility for the whole planet. That's the 'green' message of Genesis. There is a connection between human behaviour and the environment, not just for ourselves but for countless generations.

There is a spiritual dimension to the human personality

We can respond to God in a spiritual way, but we can also open ourselves up to spiritual forces that are antagonistic to God. Adam and Eve showed what men and women can do with their spiritual potential in the way they responded both to God and to the serpent who defied God.

The human family and their ancestors, Adam and Eve, possessed free will

They had the freedom to stand for or against God, just as the devil did. They had the freedom to love or to defy God. Why Adam and Eve chose to defy God we will never know. The mystery belongs to their freedom. If we could say why they did it, if we could give a reason for their rebellion, then we would prove that they weren't free at all. It's because we can't give a reason, because we can't account for their behaviour, that we can say that they were really free. They were free to go the way they chose just as the devil was free.

The rebellion of Adam and Eve has affected the whole human family

Just as we inherit our physical characteristics from our ancestors, so we also inherit our spiritual qualities from them.

There is an inherent moral flaw in the character of every single human being. No one lives up to their own moral standard. There is a gap between what we are and what we ought to be. At heart there is something wrong with all of us.

This dark side to everybody's personality does not alter

What comes out of a man is what makes him 'unclean'. For from within, out of men's hearts, come evil thoughts, sexual immorality, theft, murder, adultery, greed, malice, deceit, lewdness, envy, slander, arrogance and folly. All these evils come from inside and make a man 'unclean'.

Mark 7:20–23

the fact that we are capable of goodness and great acts of kindness. The history of the human family is landmarked by examples of great courage, altruism and sacrifice.

In fact, it is these virtues that make us different from the animal world, which is motivated entirely by instinct. Men and women also are driven by instinct but there is a conscience that will often override reactions which are based on instinct. Nevertheless, it is out of the flawed human heart that so much evil, corruption and suffering come.

Conflict with God and its consequences

The picture in the Bible is of a world that, in spite of its original goodness, is dominated and disordered by two influences, human and spiritual, that are in conflict with God.

The human level

We see the effects in war and famine. We inflict the vast majority of human suffering on ourselves. Genocide and ethnic cleansing have, throughout history to the present day, afflicted every continent. In our own time the killing fields of Cambodia and Bosnia, Sudan and Iraq have stained the conscience of the modern world.

There is enough food in the world for every mouth to be fed and for every life to be nourished. It is a matter of human responsibility that we have not yet

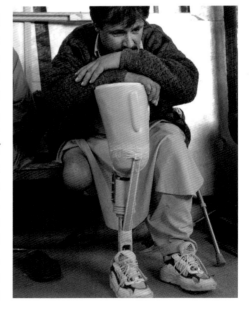

Noor Mohammad waits in line for treatment at the International Red Cross Orthopedic Centre in Kabul, Afghanistan. The Orthopedic project registers and cares for around 7,000 amputees a year, 77 per cent of whom are victims of land mines.

devised a system of feeding the whole world – in spite of possessing the most sophisticated technology in food production and communication systems.

The sight and sound of a starving baby crying at her mother's milkless breast may not immediately seem to be our responsibility. We cannot identify a single act in our own lives that has actually caused this misery, and the suffering is so far away. It is easier to blame God. Yet if the world was determined to feed the whole world, then every mouth and every belly on the face of the earth would be filled.

In spite of vast strides forward in science and technology, we have made little progress in alleviating the hideous suffering caused by famine and malnutrition. What stops it happening?

Certainly there are waves of public compassion that crash in on the shores of government. Sir Bob Geldof and Bono of U2 have stirred the popular conscience. They've harnessed the great 'M' forces of Music, the Media and Money to press the cause of greater justice for the world's poor. They've met with the leaders of the world and made the case about trade, aid and debt on behalf of the heavily indebted nations, especially in the sub-Saharan regions. Great campaigns such as Make Poverty History, Jubilee 2000 and Stop Climate Chaos have mobilized hundreds of thousands onto the streets literally to circle cities and demand action from the G8 leaders. These crusades show that the people are not without pity or power. But more is needed if the world is to change. There's widespread frustration that in spite of the public clamour for action nothing fundamental has changed. So, what stops the world really changing?

The problem lies in two places. The human heart that can love with great passion is flawed with selfishness. Although the heart can often rise above self-interest, its natural state is to favour its own interests. We can see evidence of that in families, offices, neighbourhoods and the world at large.

The gap between those who have (and who ensure that they keep on having) and those who have not (and are powerless to improve their lot) is evidence of the self-interest that possesses individuals and nations. Whatever the political solutions to so much human suffering are, be they socialist, capitalist or a mixture of both, the fact is that the cause of the suffering lies in the human heart.

Drought in Lafry, north-east Kenya. A young girl rolls a container of water home past the corpses of dead cows. The town has a newly drilled borehole with good water, but the drought has killed the pasture leaving animals with nothing to eat.

33

The spiritual level

There is another dimension. It is difficult to demonstrate because by its nature it is spiritual and invisible. If the teachings of Jesus are to be taken seriously then the world is pervaded through and through by a force that influences the way people behave.

There are many images in the Bible that describe what we have already identified as the devil. He is known as the 'Prince of Darkness'. Darkness is an appropriate picture and helps us understand the nature of the spiritual problem that causes suffering.

When a place is dark it is difficult, sometimes impossible, to be aware of other objects and people round about you. If

Sudanese refugees arrive at a refugee camp on the edge of Sudan.

you can't see them or hear them then you are blind to their needs. And, if you're blind to their needs then obviously you will not act in their interests. The darkness that shrouds the earth is one which makes people blind to the tragedies of others. It clothes their imaginations with a dark hood so that they fail to put themselves into the shoes of those who suffer.

When we fail to put ourselves into the situations of others, when our imaginations are darkened, then we fail to act to alleviate the suffering of others and to eliminate its causes.

Of course, there are times when horrific pictures appear on television and shock us and stir us to some action. The light of truth for a moment dispels the darkness. But soon the darkness envelops us again. And although we pay lip service to the scale of human tragedy, we live on untouched by the trauma suffered. We don't feel the suffering enough to become engaged in radical action.

The generator of the darkness is the one who waged war in heaven against God. His purpose is to throw the world into confusion and turmoil and to destroy what God creates.

God's plans are for goodness, healing and peace. The devil is bent on evil, suffering and destruction. The combination of a sinister spiritual power and human self-interest contributes to much of the disorder in the world and the suffering that ensues.

Although it may be appropriate to account for the suffering that comes from war and famine in this way, it's more difficult to explain why children should die of leukaemia and young adults suffer with Motor Neurone Disease.

But even here we may discover that it is the way we have abused our environment, for which we have been given responsibility by God, that has brought about these diseases.

All that is necessary for the triumph of evil is that good men do nothing.

Edmund Burke

We now know that lung cancer is very often triggered by smoking (both active and passive). Perhaps we will discover that leukaemia, for example, is something that has come about through negligent use of radiation.

But what of the tragedies that arise from natural disasters? Yet even some of these are not without an element of human responsibility. Why, for example, do people continue to live in San Francisco when it is known to be built on a fault line?

Although it is not the responsibility of children born in inhospitable parts of the world, nevertheless at some stage in the history of the human family decisions were taken that have inevitably affected subsequent generations. Just as the decisions to pollute the oceans of today will detrimentally affect the children of tomorrow.

That's the way the world is. Causes and effects.

All of this justly gives rise to the questions, 'Well, that might be how it all began, but does God have to sit back like a detached spectator? Why doesn't God do something?'

CHAPTER THREE

Why doesn't God do something?

Many people imagine that God must be like a good parent. He won't always give us what we want. But if anything bad should happen to us, then he'd be the first one there doing something about it. So why doesn't God do just that when it comes to human suffering?

How do we know God loves us?

C. S. Lewis said that it is amazing, given the extent of human suffering, that people should continue to believe God is love. The majority apparently do believe that God is loving. But the question they then want answered is why such a God doesn't do something about the state of the world, and rid the planet of all the causes of human misery.

The expectation that God should rise up and do something to rid the world of suffering implies that he must be against the evil of suffering. The hope that God should act against all the injustices in the world suggests too that he is on the side of justice. Also, the prayer that he will come and rescue us out of our misery further suggests a God who looks on us with compassion.

These intuitions that we have of God being against evil, in favour of justice and full of compassion speak of a God of love. Is that a flight of fantasy? Is there any substance to our intuition that the world is governed by a God of love? Is he good, just, merciful and loving?

The nearest we can get to knowing what God is like is to look at Jesus. When you go brass-rubbing you cover the brass with paper and rub gently with a wax crayon. As you do so the image of the now invisible brass comes through in the different substance of wax and paper. The image of the

> Jesus is the reflection of God's glory and the exact imprint of God's very being.
>
> *Hebrews 1:3*

Jesus: what others have said

Christianity will go. It will vanish and shrink. I needn't argue about that; I'm right and I will be proved right. We [the Beatles] are more popular than Jesus now; I don't know which will go first – rock 'n' roll or Christianity.

JOHN LENNON

If Jesus Christ were to come today, people would not even crucify him. They would ask him to dinner, and hear what he had to say, and make fun of it.

THOMAS CARLYLE

A man who was completely innocent, offered himself as a sacrifice for the good of others, including his enemies, and became the ransom of the world. It was a perfect act.

MAHATMA GANDHI

I know men and I tell you that Jesus Christ is no mere man. Between Him and every other person in the world there is no possible term of comparison. Alexander, Caesar, Charlemagne and I have founded empires. But on what did we rest the creation of our genius? Upon force. Jesus Christ founded His empire upon love; and at this hour millions of men would die for Him.

NAPOLEON BONAPARTE

Jesus Christ was an extremist for love, truth and goodness.

MARTIN LUTHER KING JR

I am an historian, I am not a believer, but I must confess as a historian that this penniless preacher from Nazareth is irrevocably the very centre of history. Jesus Christ is easily the most dominant figure in all history.

H. G. WELLS

invisible God comes through to us in the different substance of the flesh and blood of Jesus Christ. Jesus shows us what God is like. He helps us to see more clearly the mind of God who lives at the heart of a world that suffers.

Of all the great religious teachers to walk the earth one stands out. To note his outstanding qualities does not mean rubbishing the virtues of the others. There is a uniqueness about Jesus that compels attention.

He is the only founder of a major world religion to make, among others, the following claims:

- He had authority on earth to forgive people their sins

- He was the embodiment of truth

- He was equal with God

- His death and resurrection were a means of uniting God and the human family through the forgiveness of sins

- He would rise out of his grave

- He could give eternal life to his followers

- He had the authority to judge the world

- The worship offered by women and men is equally acceptable

- Suffering is not a punishment from God

- He would return to rid the world of evil.

If the claims listed in the box 'Sayings Of Jesus' (see page 40) are in any way false, or if they have been falsely attributed to Jesus, then the Christian faith is seriously undermined. If on the other hand these claims stand, then Jesus of Nazareth is the most important person ever to have walked the face of the earth. What he says about God, suffering and the world's destiny commands attention.

Sayings of Jesus

Know that the Son of Man has authority on earth to forgive sins.

MARK 2:10

Jesus answered, 'I am the way and the truth and the life. No-one comes to the Father except through me.'

JOHN 14:6

While they were eating, Jesus took bread, gave thanks and broke it, and gave it to his disciples, saying, 'Take and eat; this is my body.'

Then he took the cup, gave thanks and offered it to them, saying, 'Drink from it, all of you. This is my blood of the covenant, which is poured out for many for the forgiveness of sins.'

MATTHEW 26:26–28

He then began to teach them that the Son of Man must suffer many things and be rejected by the elders, chief priests and teachers of the law, and that he must be killed and after three days rise again.

MARK 8:31

He looked towards heaven and prayed: 'Father, the time has come. Glorify your Son, that your Son may glorify you. For you granted him authority over all people that he might give eternal life to all those you have given him. Now this is eternal life: that they may know you, the only true God, and Jesus Christ, whom you have sent.'

JOHN 17:1–3

Thomas said to him, 'My Lord and my God!'

Then Jesus told him, 'Because you have seen me, you have believed; blessed are those who have not seen and yet have believed.'

JOHN 20:28–29

'Do not be amazed at this, for a time is coming when all who are in their graves will hear his voice and come out – those who have done good will rise to live, and those who have done evil will rise to be condemned... my judgment is just, for I seek not to please myself but him who sent me.'

JOHN 5:28–30

Again the high priest asked him, 'Are you the Christ, the Son of the Blessed One?'

'I am,' said Jesus. 'And you will see the Son of Man sitting at the right hand of the Mighty One and coming on the clouds of heaven.'

The high priest tore his clothes, 'Why do we need any more witnesses?' he asked, 'You have heard the blasphemy. What do you think?'

MARK 14:61–63

'For God so loved the world that he gave his one and only Son, that whoever believes in him shall not perish but have eternal life.'

JOHN 3:16

Much of what Jesus taught was through stories. One of the most well known is the parable of the prodigal son, a story of love, rejection, suffering and forgiveness. It concerns a father and his two sons. The younger one asks for his share of his inheritance, and in spite of this being the same as wishing that his father were dead, he is given what he asks for.

The selfishness of the younger son leads him to disaster. In the depths of the suffering that he inflicts on himself, he comes to his senses and decides to return home.

The Return of the Prodigal Son *by P. G. Batoni, Pavlovsk Palace, St Petersburg, Russia.*

To his surprise he finds his father is waiting for him. In spite of the convention that a nobleman never runs in public, the father rushes towards him and hugs and kisses him, his heart bursting with compassion for his son. Then, to the jealous consternation of the elder brother, he throws a party to celebrate the prodigal's return.

One of the points that Jesus was making was that, in spite of the son's selfish foolishness, the father would never give up on him. Jesus holds the good father before us as a picture of God. However much we may go against God, and however much suffering we may inflict on ourselves and God's world, he will never abandon us.

Our sufferings do not drive God away from his world. Rather, the pain and the agony draw God further into the world. This dynamic involvement of God reached a climax when, in the person of Jesus Christ, he actually entered the world, took flesh and blood, and lived among us.

God became one of us 'from the womb to the tomb'. He took human flesh in the womb of Mary. She gave birth to Jesus in the crude surroundings of an outhouse in Bethlehem. He was not shielded from the pain and trauma of being born. These experiences shaped him as they do every human being.

As an infant he and his parents were robbed of the security that surrounds and supports many young families. They were forced to flee to another country because of fears that Jesus would be killed by a jealous king. They became a refugee family in Egypt.

When they returned to Nazareth and to their extended family and community Jesus grew up like every other child into adolescence. Mentally, physically, emotionally and spiritually he matured. Although we are given few details in the Gospels there is an episode in the temple where he and his parents had a strong difference of opinion. Adolescence is full of such experiences. Adjustments have to be made by both adolescent and parents, and these are not without their trials and tribulations.

As he grew up into adulthood Jesus remained single. Not sharing his life intimately with another human being meant that he endured all the frustrations and loneliness of being single. Of course, he enjoyed the advantages too. He would never have been able to embark on the adventurous life he led had he been married with the responsibility of children. But there were times when he would have felt lonely and isolated.

He knew the sadness of bereavement. When John, his first cousin, was arrested and executed Jesus felt the hollow pain of grief. John was not only a close cousin but was a friend who understood the costly nature of Jesus' own calling. When John died Jesus was bereft of a soulmate.

The emotional pain that Jesus endured intensified when his close family failed to understand what he was doing. He surrounded himself with a surrogate family of disciples and followers. When they began to desert him the pain was almost physical.

There was yet more for Jesus to endure. The suffocating sense of helplessness that you feel when false charges are brought against you by powerful people was his. He heard people, one after the other, lie about him as they levelled unjust accusations at him.

The Jewish prophet Isaiah was inspired to describe Jesus hundreds of years before he was born: 'A man of sorrows, and acquainted with grief... surely he has borne our griefs and carried our sorrows.'

There was the mental agony of anticipating the pain that lay ahead. The fear that grips the soul as you contemplate a dangerous future. Jesus was increasingly aware of the tragic events that would carry him to his fate on the cross.

In the Garden of Gethsemane he sweated drops of blood as he agonizingly prayed that the bitter cup of

> As a child I received instruction both in the Bible and in the Talmud. I am a Jew, but I am enthralled by the luminous figure of the Nazarene... No one can read the Gospels without feeling the actual presence of Jesus. His personality pulsates in every word.
>
> *Albert Einstein*

Jesus the Son of God suffers

While they were there, the time came for the baby to be born, and she gave birth to her firstborn, a son. She wrapped him in strips of cloth and placed him in a manger, because there was no room for them in the inn.

LUKE 2:6–7

When they had gone, an angel of the Lord appeared to Joseph in a dream. 'Get up,' he said, 'take the child and his mother and escape to Egypt. Stay there until I tell you, for Herod is going to search for the child to kill him.'

So he got up, took the child and his mother during the night and left for Egypt, where he stayed until the death of Herod.

MATTHEW 2:13–15

And he was in the desert for forty days, being tempted by Satan.

MARK 1:13

When Mary reached the place where Jesus was and saw him, she fell at his feet and said, 'Lord, if you had been here, my brother would not have died.'

When Jesus saw her weeping, and the Jews who had come along with her also weeping, he was deeply moved in spirit and troubled. 'Where have you laid him?' he asked.

'Come and see, Lord,' they replied.

Jesus wept.

Then the Jews said, 'See how he loved him!'

JOHN 11:32–36

Going a little farther, he fell to the ground and prayed that if possible the hour might pass from him. 'Abba, Father,' he said, 'everything is possible for you. Take this cup from me. Yet not what I will, but what you will.'

MARK 14:35–36

Now the betrayer had arranged a signal with them: 'The one I kiss is the man; arrest him and lead him away under guard.' Going at once to Jesus, Judas said, 'Rabbi!' and kissed him. The men seized Jesus and arrested him.

MARK 14:44–46

The chief priests and the whole Sanhedrin were looking for false evidence against Jesus so that they could put him to death. But they did not find any, though many false witnesses came forward.

MATTHEW 26:59–60

The soldiers led Jesus away into the palace (that is, the Praetorium) and called together the whole company of soldiers. They put a purple robe on him, then wove a crown of thorns and set it on him. And they began to call out to him, 'Hail, King of the Jews!' Again and again they struck him on the head with a staff and spat on him. Falling on their knees, they worshipped him. And when they had mocked him, they took off the purple robe and put his own clothes on him. Then they led him out to crucify him.

MARK 15:16–20

At the sixth hour darkness came over the whole land until the ninth hour. And at the ninth hour Jesus cried out in a loud voice, 'Eloi, Eloi, lama sabachthani?' – which means 'My God, my God, why have you forsaken me?'

When some of those standing near heard this, they said, 'Listen, he's calling Elijah.'

One man ran, filled a sponge with wine vinegar, put it on a stick, and offered it to Jesus to drink. 'Leave him alone now. Let's see if Elijah comes to take him down,' he said.

With a loud cry, Jesus breathed his last.

The curtain of the temple was torn in two from top to bottom. And when the centurion, who stood there in front of Jesus, heard his cry and saw how he died, he said, 'Surely this man was the Son of God!'

MARK 15:33–39

suffering might pass him by. His soul was in turmoil as he realized all that he was to go through. Like us all he prayed that God his Father would save him from the moment of agony.

All the physical pain that Jesus dreaded became real as he was led to the place of crucifixion. They whipped him, twisted a crown of thorns onto his head, spat on him, mocked him and hit him in the face. They then stretched him out on a wooden cross and impaled him.

Hoisting up the cross they left him there to hang in the midday sun. The writers of the Gospels spare the physical

details of crucifixion. When death came, bringing relief to his beaten body, it was the rib cage collapsing on the lungs that finally killed him.

As he endured the physical agony of crucifixion, Jesus experienced a spiritual torment that racked his whole being. He, who from eternity had enjoyed an intimately close relationship with God his Father, found that in his sufferings he was all alone. God seemed distant and remote from his searing pain.

Throughout his life on earth he prayed to God always as 'Father'. Now in this hour of desperation he cried out, 'My God, My God, why have you forsaken me?' There was a spiritual loneliness as he trod through the valley of the shadow of death.

When the Roman centurion heard Jesus cry out and saw him die he said, 'Surely this man was the Son of God.' What is remarkable about this observation is that it was the way Jesus suffered that led him to that conclusion. Most people might have thought this if they had seen Jesus come down from the cross miraculously. But he didn't.

He endured the suffering to the end because, as the Son of God, he was showing God's solidarity with a world in which every one of his creatures suffers. Jesus revealed something special about God – he's a suffering God standing with us in all our pain and sadnesses.

It is because God in Jesus has suffered that we know that he understands us when we hurt and cry.

But although having a God who is acquainted with our grief and sorrows is a consolation in our distress, it still leaves unanswered the question as to what he, as a God of love and power, is going to do about the disorders within his creation that cause such pain and misery. My children may well find comfort in my holding them when they get hurt, but they have a right to expect me to deal, as far as I am able, with the things that distress them.

What is God doing for his suffering creation?

An important point to bear in mind is that creation is still happening. Although God initiated an act of creation when he made the universe, he is still at work sustaining it and supplying it with all the energy for it to continue to exist.

It would be wrong to think of the world in terms of someone making something like a car which becomes totally independent of its creator. Unfortunately, that's how many people see it. They see that the car has broken down and view the work of Jesus in terms of a mechanic who comes with the manual and the spare parts to show us how to fix it.

Such a picture fails to do justice to the truth that God is involved with his creation now, as he was when he created it in an original act many years previously. If God withdrew the supply of energy from the universe which sustains it, it would shatter like an imploding light bulb.

God is at work in and through his creation like an artist, like a sculptor working with raw material. Creation is not finished. There are flaws in it, weaknesses and imperfections, which for ever present new challenges to his creative artistry. He works away at the raw material he himself has brought into being with the promise, 'I am making everything new!'

A friend of mine recalls that when she was at Art College and learning to draw, the teacher insisted that they never rubbed out a wrong line; instead they were to use the line, build on it, shape it into the picture. The mistakes were incorporated into the drawing and in the process were redeemed and turned to good. And so nothing was wasted. It is this same process which is at work in creation.

There are blemishes and flaws, there are destructive forces working against that which is good. God is for ever responding to these as he continues to create a world which one day will be free of the disorders that cause pain and

> I consider that our present sufferings are not worth comparing with the glory that will be revealed in us… creation itself will be liberated from its bondage to decay and brought into the glorious freedom of the children of God.
>
> *Romans 8:18–21*

misery. But for the moment creation is not yet finished and is full of imperfections.

We are like clay in the hands of a potter. As the wheel turns so he shapes the raw material with his fingers. The clay is not perfect but he works with it, bringing out the best in it. Just as the clay begins to assume a fine shape the thumb of the potter presses in and downwards apparently undoing all that has gone before. The potter is skilled and wiser than the onlooker, knowing the secret designs in his own mind.

He painstakingly and patiently applies himself to the task in hand. He attends to every detail and knows the quality and potential of the material. He continues to shape and to mould the clay until he is satisfied that with his hands he has wrought out of the poor raw material the best and richest pot.

For the clay it is an unnerving experience to be in the hands of the potter. The designs the clay has are different from those of the potter. Furthermore, the clay does not see that the sensitive clay-clad hands of the potter have been scarred with nails.

The clear message of Jesus echoed throughout the Bible is that the future will involve a decisive act of God against the forces of disorder that are hell-bent on destroying God's creation. At the moment God wrestles with them like an artist working with poor raw materials, bringing good out of evil. In the future God will act against them decisively. This idea is covered by the Bible's picture of God as judge.

At this point many people get cold feet. 'How can a God of love judge?' they wonder. But in fact the very question 'Why doesn't God do something about the terrible things in the world?' is a request for God to be a judge. The question expects that God will judge between good and bad and rid the world of the latter. What's being looked for is a God of judgment. And this is what Jesus promises.

When I was a teacher it was important for me to ensure that there was no cheating and bullying. If I had turned a blind eye to young people doing these things on the grounds that I was an RE teacher and couldn't possibly upset anybody the verdict on me would have been less than favourable! A caring and fair teacher would be expected to take action against those who bullied and cheated. And so it is that a loving and just God must be expected one day to take action against the dark forces of selfishness, injustice and oppression. The question is not 'How can a God of love judge?' but rather 'How can a God of love not judge?'

So when people say, 'Why doesn't God do something about the pain and misery in the world?', the Christian answer is that he will come one day to judge the world, to act decisively against all that is evil and defuse it of its power.

Those who are feeling the sharp end of suffering may well ask why God waits so long before ushering in this new era. There can be no full answer to this mystery, but the Bible does offer some hints.

Our request that God should rid the earth of all those who have had any part in contributing to the emotional and physical suffering of the world presents each of us with a problem. If we want God to judge the good and the bad and to remove all those who have hurt another human being, who do we imagine would be left? Not I.

The truth is that to a greater or lesser degree we've all had some part in adding to the pain and suffering of the world. What we should be asking for is not so much for God to judge the earth but for God to have mercy on us all.

And in fact that's the fullest revelation that the Bible gives us of God – he is both our judge and our saviour; the God of justice and of mercy. He will act against all that is selfish, unjust and oppressive and he will also have mercy on those who come under his judgment.

The reason that God waits so long to exercise his judgment over the world and act against all that is evil is that he wants us to think again about our lives and to open ourselves up to his mercy. It is through receiving his mercy that we avoid his judgment.

The greatest insight into God's plans for the world come to us through Jesus. His name contains the greatest clue – it means 'God saves'. Throughout the Old Testament God promised to save his people from the effects of selfishness, injustice and oppression. It was a promise of salvation that was never fully realized. When Jesus came he claimed the authority of God to forgive people, to save them from their sins. (In a later chapter we shall explore this more fully.) Jesus occupies the central place in God's plans for the earth. Through his innocent death on the cross he offers forgiveness to the whole world and a unique opportunity to experience the mercy of God.

It is Jesus who saves us from the judgment of God, which is the ultimate consequence of our selfishness. The God of love will act against all causes of suffering, which means he will act against us. But the God of love has also shown us his mercy by sending Jesus to save us from our sins and their fatal consequences.

'But God demonstrated his own love for us in this: While we were still sinners, Christ died for us' (Romans 5:8).

> But do not forget this one thing, dear friends: With the Lord a day is like a thousand years, and a thousand years are like a day. The Lord is not slow in keeping his promise, as some understand slowness. He is patient with you, not wanting anyone to perish, but everyone to come to repentance.
>
> *2 Peter 3:8–9*

51

CHAPTER FOUR

Where is God?

Often it's only when disaster strikes that we start praying in earnest. We forget all the arguments for and against the existence of God and cry out for God to help us. But if in spite of our prayers the pain continues, then either we doubt the existence of God or we wonder what sort of a God he really is. That makes our suffering all the more unbearable. Why doesn't God say something? Is he there? Doesn't he care?

God suffers when we get hurt

When someone you love deeply gets hurt you feel it yourself. You put yourself in their shoes, and you imagine what they must be going through. You take their pain to yourself. The sensation is almost physical – their grief is your grief, their suffering is your suffering. Even though the person may be hundreds of miles away you feel at one with them in their tragedy. Such is the power of love and the power of the imagination.

God himself is at one with us when we suffer. Just as a good parent is caught up in the life of their children, so God is attentive to us. He's straining forward, flinching at every scar and reeling at every wound we endure. Through the power of his imagination he puts himself into our situations and weeps with those who weep. Even though God may be over and above us in heaven, he is also with us – so when we suffer he suffers.

For most of us pain comes and goes throughout our lives. There are times of endurance and times of relief. But because God is intimately involved with every single one of his creatures there is a sense in which his pain is relentless and never-ending. While any single one of his creatures is in pain, God is in pain. His suffering is greater than we can ever imagine, for it is multiplied by the number of people who are suffering.

Jesus once said: 'Look at these two sparrows. They're worth very little. But not one of them will fall to the ground without your Father being there. Listen. You're worth a lot more to God than the birds of the air.' Jesus was showing us that if God was involved with the suffering of the birds that he'd made we could be absolutely sure that he would be with us in all our pain and suffering.

When God the Father experienced the death of Jesus, his Son, he himself plumbed the depths of tragedy. The

The Suffering God

A God who cannot suffer is poorer than any man. For a God who is incapable of suffering is a being who cannot be involved. Suffering and injustice do not affect him. And because he is so completely insensitive, he cannot be affected or shocked by anything. He cannot weep, for he has no tears. But the one who cannot suffer cannot love either.

JÜRGEN MOLTMANN

The only credible theology for Auschwitz is one that makes God an inmate of the place.

KENNETH SURIN

Suffering is the heritage of the bad, of the penitent, and of the Son of God. Each one ends in the cross. The bad thief is crucified, the penitent thief is crucified, and the Son of God is crucified. By these signs we know the widespread heritage of suffering.

OSWALD CHAMBERS

Only the suffering God can help.

DIETRICH BONHOEFFER

There was a cross in the heart of God before there was one planted on the green hill outside Jerusalem. And now that the cross of wood has been taken down, the one in the heart of God abides, and it will remain so long as there is one sinful soul for whom to suffer.

C. A. DINSMORE

death of Jesus on the cross was brutal and painful. But it's often overlooked that God the Father was also heartbroken with grief as he was cut off from his Son.

There was once an earthquake in which a city was devastated. Houses collapsed like packs of cards. Hospitals switched to emergency procedures, and doctors and nurses sped to their posts. News was coming in all the time of appalling casualties.

A school had caved in, killing all the teachers and most of the children. A little boy, badly maimed, was rescued from the rubble and rushed to hospital. For hours a team of doctors and nurses fought to save his life while his mother waited anxiously outside the operating theatre. After seven hours of painstaking surgery the little boy died.

Instead of leaving it to a nurse to tell the mother the surgeon went himself. As he broke the dreadful news, the mother became hysterical in her grief and attacked the surgeon, pummelling his chest with her fists. But instead of pushing her away, the doctor held her to himself tightly until the woman's

God is love. That is why he suffers. To love our suffering sinful world is to suffer... The one who does not see God's suffering, does not see his love. So, suffering is down at the centre of things, deep down where the meaning is. Suffering is the meaning of our world. For love is the meaning. And love suffers. The tears of God are the meaning of history.

Nicholas Wolterstorff

The aftermath of an earthquake in Armenia in 1989.

55

sobbing subsided and she rested cradled in his arms.

And then in the heavy silence the surgeon began to weep. Tears streamed down his face and grief racked his body. For he had come to the hospital the moment he heard that his one and only son had been killed in the same school.

Just as the surgeon knew the sorrow and grief of the bereaved mother, so God the Father is acquainted intimately with our griefs and sorrows.

Even when he's silent, God is there

In the painting by Paul Gauguin called *Human Misery* there are two people in the foreground looking sad and dejected. A wall cuts through the scene diagonally and beyond it stands a figure looking on. It speaks to me of the unhappiness in the world and the sense that God is distant and remote, as if on the other side of the wall.

I believe in love even when I don't feel it.
I believe in God even when He is silent.

Words found penned on the wall of a prison cell in Europe

When in a time of trouble we start praying, there is no sense that he is listening, let alone answering our prayers. The silence of God makes our unhappiness all the more difficult to cope with. It can lead us to wonder whether God has abandoned us.

But down the years as people have wrestled with the problem of suffering, new reflections have been offered on the silence and inaction of God. God is still there, standing by us when we suffer, but through his silence he is making way for others to draw near to us.

I remember once walking past the school at the end of our road. On the other side of the six-foot wall I could hear a small child crying inconsolably. A teacher was trying to comfort her but with little immediate success. Like any parent, the sound of a child sobbing stirred my heart.

As I walked on down the road with the child's crying ringing in my ears, I stopped dead in my tracks as I realized

The Long Silence

At the end of time billions of people were scattered on a great plane before God's throne. Most shrank back from the brilliant light before them. But some groups near the front talked heatedly – not with cringing shame, but with belligerence.

'Can God judge us? How can he know about suffering?' snapped a young woman. She ripped open a sleeve to reveal a tattooed number from a Nazi concentration camp. 'We endured terror, beatings, torture and death!'

In another group, a black boy lowered his collar. 'What about this?' he demanded, showing an ugly rope burn. 'Lynched – for no crime but being black.'

In another crowd, there was a pregnant schoolgirl with sullen eyes. 'Why should I suffer?' she murmured. 'It wasn't my fault.'

Far out across the plane there were hundreds of such groups. Each had a complaint against God for the evil and suffering he had permitted in his world. How lucky God was to live in heaven where all was sweetness and light, where there was no weeping or fear, no hunger or hatred. What did God know of all that man had been forced to endure, in this world? For God leads a pretty sheltered life, they said.

So each of these groups sent forth their leader, chosen because he or she had suffered the most. A Jew, a black, someone from Hiroshima, a horribly deformed arthritic, a thalidomide child. In the centre of the plane they consulted with each other. At last they were ready to present their case. It was rather clever.

Before God could be qualified to be their judge, he must endure what they had endured. The decision was that God should be sentenced to live upon earth – as a human!

'Let him be born a Jew. Let the legitimacy of his birth be doubted. Give him a work so difficult that even his family will think him out of his mind when he tries to do it. Let him be betrayed by his closest friends. Let him face charges, be tried by a prejudiced jury, and convicted by a cowardly judge. Let him be tortured. At the last, let him see what it means to be terribly alone. Then let him die. Let him die so that there can be no doubt that he died. Let there be a host of witnesses to verify it.'

As each leader announced his portion of the sentence, loud murmurs of approval went up from the throng of people assembled. And when the last had finished pronouncing sentence there was a long silence. No one uttered another word. No one moved. For suddenly all knew that God had already served his sentence.

ANONYMOUS

that the child who was in tears was my own daughter. Part of me wanted to vault over the wall and rescue her – to tell her that it was all right, that Daddy was here and she'd be OK now. But another part of me knew that I should do nothing of the kind – that I had to leave her so that others could come near to her and help her.

If every time she got into difficulty I jumped in to rescue

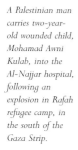

A Palestinian man carries two-year-old wounded child, Mohamad Awni Kulab, into the Al-Najjar hospital, following an explosion in Rafah refugee camp, in the south of the Gaza Strip.

her, how would she ever grow and mature as a person? I walked on down the road by the side of the wall with a very heavy heart.

In the silence of God

If, every time we encountered difficulties, we were able to make them vanish like melting snow then it is likely that we would never mature. We would remain as infants who see the world with themselves at the centre, and simply shout and scream until we got what we wanted.

It's when our own plans are frustrated that we are forced to consider the world from other perspectives, and to realize that it is not we who stand at the centre of the universe.

It's this coming of age, this maturing, which happens when God is often silent to our pleas. He's still there. Listening. Empathizing. Feeling. Loving. But for our own good, which we can't possibly see or imagine, he keeps his own counsel for the time being.

The apostle Paul tells us that he begged God to rescue him from suffering. In his second letter to the Corinthians he wrote, 'Three times I pleaded with the Lord to take it away from me. But he said to me, "My grace is sufficient for you, for my power is made perfect in weakness." Therefore I will boast all the more gladly about my weaknesses, so that Christ's power may rest on me. That is why, for Christ's sake, I delight in weaknesses, in insults, in hardships, in persecutions, in difficulties. For when I am weak, then I am strong' (2 Corinthians 12:8–10).

And again, in his letter to the Romans he says, 'we also rejoice in our sufferings, because we know that suffering produces perseverance; perseverance, character; and character, hope. And hope does not disappoint us, because God has poured out his love into our hearts by the Holy Spirit, whom he has given us' (Romans 5:3–5).

> As cold as everything looks in winter, the sun has not forsaken us. He has only drawn away for a little, for good reasons, one of which is that we may learn that we cannot do without him.
>
> *George MacDonald*

> Deep unspeakable suffering may well be called a baptism, a regeneration, the initiation into a new state.
>
> *George Eliot*

This is a well-worn path that many saints have trodden. It was through enduring difficulties that Paul experienced God and grew as a person. Sometimes God does dramatically answer our prayers and miraculously rescues us out of our troubles. But there are other times when he chooses instead to give us the grace to endure, because that's how we are to mature.

Only a tyrant doesn't feel pain

There's a Chinese tale about an elderly couple who longed for a child. After years of barrenness a baby was conceived. The day before the infant was born, a genie visited the parents and granted them one wish for their child.

They thought long and hard. When the genie returned the parents were in no doubt. 'We wish that our child may never feel any pain.' The genie begged them to think again. 'No,' he pleaded, 'anything, anything but that.' But the parents insisted and so their wish was granted.

Fortunately they didn't live long enough to see their child grow up to become the greatest tyrant in the land. Only a tyrant doesn't feel the pain of others.

Jesus revealed to the world that God, far from being an unfeeling tyrant, loves us like a good father and feels every wound we suffer.

CHAPTER FIVE

A punishment from God?

One of the commonest reactions to unexpected suffering is that it may be a punishment from God. We inevitably go in search of reasons, or for somebody to blame. These ideas dominate the first thoughts of most of us when we suffer.

Whose side is God on?

Often when things begin to go badly wrong we wonder if God is punishing us for something we've done. It's a primitive and irrational thought. It starts with us asking 'Why me?' 'Why is this happening to me?' Because we cannot find any human explanation we imagine that there must be some other mysterious reason.

When this question is coupled with us asking God to help us it's not long before we begin to think that he must be behind the suffering we're going through. The question then returns, 'But why me?' 'Why is God doing this to me?' We start to look at ourselves.

Because we're all less than perfect we soon become aware of many of the wrong things that we've said, thought and done. Perhaps one or two things in particular stand out that we're ashamed of. Even with only a little knowledge of God we can imagine his reactions. We go on to think that out of his displeasure he has decided to lay this suffering on us to teach us a lesson. It's quite natural to think like this. Most of us do. But Jesus through his teaching makes us think again.

God beneath the rubble

In 1966 disaster struck a mining village in Wales called Aberfan. Shortly after the children had assembled in the school the nearby towering slag heap collapsed on top of them. Teachers and children were killed in an appalling tragedy.

Some years later W. H. Vanstone reflected on where God was on that fateful morning: 'We believe that at the moment when the mountain of Aberfan slipped, "something went wrong". Our faith is in a Creator who does not abandon even this, nor those who suffered, wept and died in it. Our preaching on the Sunday after the tragedy was not of a God who, from the top of the mountain, caused or permitted, for his own inscrutable reasons, its disruption and descent; but of one who received, at the foot of the mountain, its appalling impact and who, in the extremity of endeavour, will find yet new resources to restore and to redeem.'

When people have a narrow escape from a tragedy they will sometimes say something like, 'Somebody up there was looking after me' or 'I must have had a guardian angel' or 'I reckon God was with me'.

After the terrible 7/7 terrorist attacks in London when over fifty people lost their lives, the media were full of heart-rending stories of the impact the devastation had had. It was a day of heroic struggle as the injured helped one another in the tunnel of destruction and the emergency services risked their own lives to rescue the maimed and dying. As with 9/11, there were poignant messages on mobile phones and stories of lines going dead mid-conversation. In the aftermath and to this day remarkable people are literally remaking their lives with remade limbs and extraordinary courage. Those who've lost loved ones are still coming to terms with their loss and their feelings towards the assassins – some say they can forgive, others that it is impossible to forgive the murder of their beloved. Although the crime was motivated by a fanatical interpretation of Islam, the toll of dead and injured

Aberfan - the school that died in a sea of mud. An aerial view of the scene of the disaster where a sea of mud and coal dust smashed through the school and a row of houses on 21 October 1966. 144 people were killed, 116 of whom were children.

included Muslims as well as Christians and Jews, people of other faiths and no faith at all. Understandably, those who escaped death on that day talked about thanking God for being alive. There were many stories of people who for various reasons missed the bus or the train.

I remember hearing one person who escaped a disaster say, 'I guess God was on my side.' But if God was on his side and on the side of all who escaped, does that mean

A citizen of London signs a memorial message at St Pancras Church near Euston Station after a two-minute silence in memory of the victims of the London bomb attack on 7 July 2005.

that God took sides against those who died?

This sort of view reinforces the idea that suffering must be a punishment from God for things that people have done wrong. But if that really is the reason for suffering it certainly doesn't explain why the good die young and why so many innocent children also suffer. The truth is that God is on the side of those who suffer *and* those who escape. He doesn't favour only one group.

A Father's grief

I had decided that I would ask the nursing staff to move all the tubes attached to Tim to the far side of the bed and then move him over from the centre of the bed to the far side. This would give me space to lie down on the near side of the bed next to Tim and to hold him closely, as I had so desperately wanted to do all that week.

I removed my leather jacket and gently got on to the bed and lay down next to our son. For the first time since early Saturday morning I was able to make proper contact with him, and I put my left arm across his chest with the fingers of my left hand around the upper part of his right arm. I put my lips to his swollen cheek and kissed him many times. I then kissed him many more times on his lips. While I was so close to him, I bade Tim my lasting and loving farewells. As I did so, I sobbed openly, with every fibre of my body aching agonizingly for this sons of ours to rest in peace, free from pain for all eternity. I told him I did not know what I was going to do without him, that the gap he would leave in his family's life would be huge and yawning.

After perhaps five minutes, Nurse Colfer knocked gently on the door, opened it slightly and asked if they could come back into the room. I asked for a few moments more to recover my composure. Getting off the bed was agonizing because I knew this was to be the last time I would hold my son properly, until the next life.

COLIN PARRY, TIM'S FATHER

Jesus said, '...not one of them shall fall to the ground without your Father.' Just as Colin held Tim, his child, on that hospital bed, so God is with us when we suffer.

How Jesus saw suffering

Jesus gained a reputation for healing people. Consequently hundreds flocked to him in all sorts of conditions. Never once did Jesus ever say that their suffering was a means of God punishing them.

Once it was put to Jesus that a man was born blind as a result of some sin on the part of him or his parents. Jesus explained that the man was blind not to punish him or his family, but to show God at work in his life.

Jesus then healed him. He mixed mud with his own saliva, put it in the man's eyes, and told him to go and wash in a certain pool. When the man had done this, he told the people who knew him as a blind beggar that Jesus had made him see.

All the religions of the world are an attempt to come to terms with the relationship between the experience of suffering and the existence of God. There are many religious traditions that hold to the view that suffering is something that God deliberately inflicts on us as a form of punishment. But the unique contribution that Jesus makes to the debate is to insist that God does not deal with us like that.

Whatever we may feel intuitively about our own lack of goodness and God's displeasure at the selfishness in the world (and according to Christian teaching these are both right insights), there is no connection to be made between them when we come to an explanation of our sufferings.

God does not strut about like a peeved deity throwing tantrums and deliberately hurting those who fail to keep the commandments. The thrust of the Bible's message is that through human history God has been unfolding a plan – rescuing us from the evil and tragedy that afflicts all of his creation. It's a story of salvation, the opposite of punishment. He's committed to healing us, not to destroying us.

As the prophet Jeremiah said when the people of Israel deliberately turned away from God: 'For I know the plans I have for you,' declares the Lord, 'plans to prosper you and not to harm you, plans to give you hope and a future' (Jeremiah 29:11).

We bring some suffering on ourselves

With advances in medical science a lot of previously inexplicable diseases are now understood. We know, for example, that if you eat an excess of fat and sugar you're much more likely to suffer coronary disease. There is a clear connection between what we do to our bodies and the diseases we suffer. As the saying goes, 'We are what we eat.'

At one stage these conditions were a mystery. It seemed quite arbitrary as to who should get lung cancer or have a heart attack. In that state of ignorance there is even more of a temptation to blame God for what is happening to someone.

In our own lifetime we have seen extraordinary

AIDS sufferer Margarette Shenge sits in her home in Nqbeni, southern Natal province South Africa. Shenge's husband died of the disease and two of her four children are also infected. Several of her children have left, leaving Shenge alone in the rural village.

Smokestacks belch plumes of brown and grey smoke into the atmosphere. Norilsk pumps out 8 per cent of all the air pollution in Russia – more than two million tons of pollutants a year, primarily sulfur dioxide.

achievements in medical science. When the HIV/AIDS epidemic first struck it seemed inconceivable that we would find a drug to combat it. Although the disease is still a worldwide threat there are now medications that arrest its advance. As medical research continues hopefully we fill find cures for this and other diseases such as Motor Neurone.

It could be that we will discover that the causes of many diseases lie with what we have been doing to our environment. Polluting the earth, poisoning the oceans, contaminating the earth, destroying biodiversity and undermining the eco-system all affect the fragile balance of life of which humanity is a part. We cannot damage the natural world with impunity. As the Bible says, we reap what we sow.

So much human suffering and tragedy is caused directly

The risk of love

A father had two children. He said he loved them very much. He was troubled by the evil influence in the world and wanted to protect his children. He was worried that as they grew up they might come under the influence of people who would lead them astray, and he couldn't bear the thought of them breaking loose and possibly making the wrong decisions. He dreaded that they might come to some harm. Such was his 'love' that he wanted to ensure that they would never suffer.

So he decided what to do. Every day he would escort them to and from school where he was happy to entrust them to the safe keeping of teachers. But as soon as they got home he locked the door, forbade the watching of television, and refused either to let them go out or to have friends in.

When the children rose up and protested, he assured them that he was doing this for the best because he 'loved' them. Was this love or tyranny?

True love gives people freedom. That freedom is dangerous. It does mean that the person loved may choose not to return the love and may go off in another direction. That's the risk inherent in love. It's the risk inherent in the way that God has made us love and loves us.

by human error. On a global scale where so much agony is due to famine and poverty, it's important to see that there is enough food to feed everybody, yet this food is not equally distributed. The problem is that the human family, especially its leaders who hold the power, is not yet determined enough to change the situation.

In the sense that God has set up the world, with its causes and effects, it could be argued that it's all his responsibility and even all his fault when something goes wrong. The alternative would be that whenever anything went wrong God would intervene and stop the causes having their natural effect.

So if, for example, the leaders of an aggressive country declared war on a weaker state then God would intervene and rob them of their freedom to choose to do such a thing.

> Earth provides enough to satisfy every man's need, but not every man's greed.
>
> *Mahatma Gandhi*

69

What's at stake in this scenario is human freedom or, as it's also known, free will.

God could end all the suffering that human beings inflict on one another in an instant. He could step in and eliminate all the pain. All that he would have to do is remove from all of us the ability to do it, that freedom to choose.

If God were to cut the free will out of our hearts we would, of course, change radically. We would cease to be human beings. We would become more like automata. We would be programmed to do exactly what he told us to do. There would be no debate, no argument, no disagreement, no disobedience, no discord, no problems, no disease, no pain, no suffering. We would be perfect – robots. And also, there would be no love.

Love and freedom go together. Love is only love when we are free to choose to please someone. The moment you are forced to do what another person asks, that is not love. Love is when someone of their own free will chooses to love and to please the other. That is how God loves us. Out of love for us he gives us the freedom to love him or not.

The freedom that God gives us is a genuine freedom. It comes from his sheer love for us. He longs for us to return his love. But he cannot and will not force us to do so.

He gives us free will. He allows us to make our own choices. And he insists that in an ordered world of cause and effect we must live with the consequences of our actions. For it is only through the consequences and results of our choices that we become fully aware of the moral quality of the decisions we take. Otherwise the world would become an even more chaotic place than it already is.

As a religious columnist for London's *The Times* once wrote, 'A world in which accidents do not happen would be so different from the actual world as to be unrecognizable. If all air crashes were miraculously soft ones, there would scarcely be any need for runways; if all aircraft engines were

> **I am condemned to be free.**
>
> *Jean-Paul Sartre*

divinely guaranteed against fault, there would be no need to service them. And if planes flew on after their engines or wings failed or fell off, there would be no need for engines or wings in the first place. The performance of one tiny miracle, provided it could be relied on, would so destroy the underlying principle of causality as to transform the world into a completely irrational state. What need or possibility would there then be for human intelligence? What chance, even, of appreciating the occasional miracle?'

To know that we are free and that we live in a world of cause and effect is no consolation to us in a time of suffering. It's like giving a lecture to a scalded child about not playing near the cooker. All the child wants and needs is comfort and help.

Nor is it helpful at that moment to try to find out whose fault the accident was – the child's or the adult's. Such is the inadequacy of looking at theories about the cause of human suffering.

In the story of the healing of the blind man, when Jesus

With God nothing is wasted

Imagine a master painter who is also a father. As he works on his canvas he is surrounded by his children, who are sometimes wayward and sometimes compliant with his wishes.

The artist has in his mind the image which through his paints he is realizing on the canvas.

As he works patiently and painstakingly he is constantly interrupted by his children putting their fingers in the paint and making their own impressions on the canvas.

So brilliant, so determined, so compassionate an artist is he that he works with their gratuitous intrusions, incorporating them into the masterpiece he is creating. Far from diminishing the outcome they even add to the texture and to the depth of the painting. Nothing is wasted.

was faced with somebody suffering and pressed to say whose fault it was, he concerned himself with the present rather than the past. He quickly dismissed the idea that the blindness was a punishment from God for the sins of either parents or child.

Beyond that he did not explore the cause of the blindness. Instead, he worked with the present situation and saw it as an opportunity for God to work in the life of the blind man and of his family and community.

This brings us back to an earlier chapter when we saw that God's work in creation has not stopped. He is continually working with the raw material of creation, wrestling with its imperfections and bringing good out of evil.

The way Jesus, the Son of God, made an ointment out of saliva and clay and applied its healing properties to the man's eyes was in itself a picture of God working with the raw materials of his creation.

The end in sight is of a universe in a state of wholeness, blemishes removed, and at one with the Creator. This is what the Hebrew word *shalom* means. Peace.

> The will of God is never exactly what you expect it to be. It may seem to be much worse, but in the end it's going to be a lot better and a lot bigger.
>
> *Elisabeth Elliot*

The miracle that Jesus performed on the blind man was simply a sign that whatever caused his blindness it was certainly not God. The miracle showed that in and through Jesus the creative work of God was continuing. And it continues to this day through the Spirit of Jesus at work in the world.

We are free to run with him, to ignore him, or even to resist him. Opening ourselves up to him will not safeguard us against the traumas and tribulations of being human, but it will ensure that as God enters our every situation he will be transforming it to bring good out of bad. Peace, not punishment, is his code of practice.

CHAPTER SIX

Jesus: the good die young

The life of Jesus is the story of a good man who suffered and died young. He was drawn to people who suffered. Like all sympathetic people he suffered much himself. Although he was the Son of God he escaped none of the trauma of being human. When the time came for him to suffer cruelly on the cross, he gave us the greatest example of the transformation of human suffering into something that was divinely good. And what happened to him after death gave a new perspective to the sufferings of the world.

Suffering through guilt

Guilt is not a fashionable word at the beginning of the twenty-first century. It's the sort of thing we send people to psychiatrists for! Guilt is a neurosis for which the doctors prescribe treatment. But guilt is a universal phenomenon and the cause of much mental and spiritual suffering.

> From the body of one guilty deed a thousand ghostly fears and haunting thoughts proceed.
>
> *William Wordsworth*

We all know what it's like to have said or done something wrong and to be troubled by it. Our conscience tells us one thing and we decide to do the opposite. Mostly it's little things that others are unaware of. Sometimes it's something more major and looms large in our thinking.

The guilt we feel robs us of our peace and leaves us restless and even anxious. We don't feel any less guilty either by talking about it or by keeping silent. We can take pills for it, receive counselling, but still it will not go away. Even if the person we have offended tells us that it's all forgotten the pain remains. We are afflicted by a dis-ease of guilt and peacelessness.

An anonymous woman wrote to a newspaper about the guilt she had suffered since having an abortion: 'Ten years on I am still waiting for forgiveness to arrive.'

There is a moving story about Jesus being approached by a woman who had done something wrong. The respectable people surrounding Jesus were scandalized that he should let the woman near him. The woman was in great distress but knew intuitively that she should come to Jesus for help.

What she heard him say was the only antidote to the guilt she suffered from what she had done wrong. 'Your sins are forgiven.' Forgiveness was the only way to deal with her guilt and Jesus knew it.

> **Every guilty person is his own hangman.**
>
> *Seneca*

Those words rang in her ears and outraged those who listened. Who was this person who even forgave sin? They knew that there was only one who had the authority to forgive people, and that was God.

But undeterred by their objection Jesus said to the woman, 'Go in peace.' In this encounter Jesus showed the entire human family that the way to inner peace comes only through forgiveness.

We do not know what the woman's sense of guilt was. Her example stands for us all. Whatever the thought, the word, the action that fills us with guilt and robs us of peace, only the forgiveness of God will be sufficient to remove the guilt and the suffering.

A story of guilt and peace

Now one of the Pharisees invited Jesus to have dinner with him, so he went to the Pharisee's house and reclined at the table. When a woman who had lived a sinful life in that town learned that Jesus was eating at the Pharisee's house, she brought an alabaster jar of perfume, and as she stood behind him at his feet weeping, she began to wet his feet with her tears. Then she wiped them with her hair, kissed them and poured perfume on them.

When the Pharisee who had invited him saw this, he said to himself, 'If this man were a prophet, he would know who is touching him and what kind of woman she is – that she is a sinner.'

Jesus answered him, 'Simon, I have something to tell you.'

'Tell me, teacher,' he said.

'Two men owed money to a certain money-lender. One owed him five hundred denarii, and the other fifty. Neither of them had the money to pay him back, so he cancelled the debts of both. Now which of them will love him more?'

Simon replied, 'I suppose the one who had the bigger debt cancelled.'

'You have judged correctly,' Jesus said.

Then he turned towards the woman and said to Simon, 'Do you see this woman? I came into your house. You did not give me any water for my feet, but she wet my feet with her tears and wiped them with her hair. You did not give me a kiss, but this woman, from the time I entered, has not stopped kissing my feet. You did not put oil on my head, but she has poured perfume on my feet. Therefore, I tell you, her many sins have been forgiven – for she loved much. But he who has been forgiven little loves little.'

Then Jesus said to her, 'Your sins are forgiven.'

The other guests began to say among themselves, 'Who is this who even forgives sin?'

Jesus said to the woman, 'Your faith has saved you; go in peace.'

LUKE 7:36–50

Healing the whole person

The readiness of Jesus to offer forgiveness is one of the most startling aspects of his life. It sets him apart in the comparative study of religion for there is no other religious leader on earth who has ever offered such forgiveness to strangers.

This unique claim of Jesus to have the authority to forgive people points up two things. It shows how different he is from the rest of us and suggests a special relationship with God. And it demonstrates that when he is confronted with someone who's suffering Jesus is concerned with the whole person, not just the body, but the dis-eased soul too.

In another episode, a paralyzed man was brought by his friends to Jesus. They could not get through the crowd, so they made a hole in the roof of the building and lowered him through it. Jesus realized that they had faith and told the man that his sins were forgiven.

Some of the community leaders were taken aback, because they knew that only God can forgive sins. This meant that Jesus was blaspheming. But Jesus was emphatic that he had the authority on earth to forgive sins. As God's Son he had the authority of his Father in heaven.

To prove his authority to forgive sins, Jesus told the man to get up, take his mat and go home. He did!

In forgiving the man's sins Jesus went to the heart of the human personality. This is where the fundamental disorder within creation lies. We are not what we would like to be nor what we sense we ought to be. In the gap between our real selves and our ideal selves there is a lot of deception and a lot of pain.

Whether the sick man's guilt was the cause of his paralysis we do not know. But the needs of the able-bodied and the disabled are all alike. The man needed to hear and experience the forgiveness of God. 'Son, your sins are forgiven' was the medicine that Jesus prescribed for his soul.

But Jesus did not stop there. He was not interested in just saving a person's soul. As God's representative on earth he wanted to show that God was still at work in and with his creation, making all things new.

He told the man: 'Get up, take your mat and go home.' The physical cure astounded everybody. Here was a man healed in both body and soul. Jesus brought healing to the whole person. This incident holds before us a pattern of God's commitment to his suffering world. His plan is to bring healing to both the spiritual and the physical realms.

Looking up at a Search and Rescue coastguard helicopter as the winchman takes a casualty up from danger to safety.

Healing through suffering

Jesus posed an important question in the controversy over forgiveness. 'Which is easier; to say to the paralytic, "Your sins are forgiven," or to say, "Get up, take your mat and walk"?' (Mark 2:9).

Most people would probably answer that 'Your sins are forgiven,' is the easier thing to say. After all, to say to someone who is paralyzed 'Get up,' would be much more risky. The likelihood is that there would be no effect at all, the man would remain paralyzed and we would have egg on our face. The advantage of saying to someone 'Your sins are forgiven,' is that there is no objective standard by which anybody else can measure whether what we said was true.

The easier thing for Jesus to say would have been 'Get up.' The hardest thing for him to say was 'Your sins are forgiven.' To say that was to commit himself to the death on the cross that would bring about the forgiveness of sins. Jesus knew that his mission would involve him in a cruel death. When he claimed authority to forgive people it was based on the sacrifice that he was soon to make on the cross.

When God sent his Son into the world he knew its

deepest need. He knew that in spite of its many different problems, what the world needed was not an economist, a politician, an environmentalist or even a good teacher but a saviour, a forgiver, someone who would rescue people from the destructive power of their own selfishness.

As the angel told the shepherds on the night Jesus was born: 'I bring you good news of great joy that will be for all people. Today in the town of David a Saviour has been born to you: he is Christ the Lord' (Luke 2:10–11).

The value of Jesus' life lay in his death and resurrection even more than in his miracles and in his teaching – what he was and did rather than what he said. His death and the suffering that he would endure as he carried the sins of the world were predicted centuries before by the prophets in the Old Testament.

When we unite ourselves to the Spirit of Jesus today we do so conscious that his life on earth was as unsoiled by sin as ours is spoiled by selfishness. The act of committing ourselves to him involves us in admitting our own lack of goodness and asking him to forgive us.

To say such a prayer, however tentatively, places us under the authority of Jesus. As we pray, so he forgives – 'your sins are forgiven'. With these words he washes us clean of all that stains us. God comes to us in a new way, filling our lives with his forgiving and life-giving Spirit.

The important point to see is that it was through the suffering of Jesus that God brought about our forgiveness. It is the greatest example in the history of the world of God taking something evil – the betrayal of Jesus by Judas and the cruel death of crucifixion – and through it bringing about something wholly good, the salvation of the world.

It gives us hope that God can transform the bleak moments of our existence, throwing light on them with his presence. This is the way that God works with his world. He is the alchemist who out of base metals produces gold.

> But he was pierced for our transgressions, he was crushed for our iniquities; the punishment that brought us peace was upon him, and by his wounds we are healed. We all, like sheep, have gone astray, each of us has turned to his own way; and the Lord has laid on him the iniquity of us all.
>
> *Isaiah 53:5–6*

In a small part of the Middle East, there is a time-honoured way of making exotic, fabulously expensive carpets. The canvas is suspended vertically, from the ceiling to the floor. The designer sits on one side, the weavers on the other. The designer has the piles of beautifully coloured wool.

The pattern is on both sides of the canvas. The designer

> It is the confession, not the priest, that gives us absolution.
>
> *Oscar Wilde*

Healing through the suffering of Jesus

Jesus did nothing wrong in his life even when he got angry. When he died on the cross he died not for his own sin but carrying the sins of the world. Even as he died he prayed that God his Father would forgive the people who had driven him there. Here is a selection of descriptions of Jesus and what he achieved through dying on the cross.

The next day John saw Jesus coming towards him and said, 'Look, the Lamb of God, who takes away the sin of the world!'

JOHN 1:29

For God so loved the world that he gave his one and only Son, that whoever believes in him shall not perish but have eternal life. For God did not send his Son into the world to condemn the world, but to save the world through him.

JOHN 3:16–17

I am the good shepherd. The good shepherd lays down his life for the sheep.

JOHN 10:11

He himself bore our sins in his body on the tree, so that we might die to sins and live for righteousness; by his wounds you have been healed... For Christ died for sins once for all, the righteous for the unrighteous, to bring you to God.

I PETER 2:24; 3:18

... the Lord Jesus Christ, who gave himself for our sins to rescue us from the present evil age, according to the will of our God and Father, to whom be glory for ever and ever. Amen.

GALATIANS 1:3–5

threads the wool through to the weavers, who carefully thread it back, working with the designer and with one another as together they develop a work of patient and beautiful craftsmanship.

An Iraqi worker weaves a carpet with a picture of the ancient human-headed winged bull at the factories of State Company for Handmade Carpets in Baghdad.

But if they don't – if, for whatever reason, the weavers fail to work with the designer or with one another – what then? If the designer is not up to the job, there's chaos.

But if the designer is sufficiently skilful then he takes the wool, wherever the weavers push it through the canvas, and

threads it back to them in a way in which not only invites and encourages them to work with him again, but continues to develop a pattern at the same time.

To believe in the God of the resurrection is to cling to the hope, against all the odds, that God will bring life out of death, and order even out of chaos.

Suffering and eternity

The resurrection of Jesus shows us that there is life beyond the crematorium. He died and was buried and on the third day he rose again. He shows us that all that is experienced in this life is lived against a backdrop called eternity. However real and awful suffering is, the Bible makes it clear that it is limited to this side of the grave. In that sense, all our sufferings are temporary. Pain, grief, death and tears will not touch us on the other side.

If we lose sight of eternity, we lose a proper sense of proportion about all that we do and endure in this life. This existence becomes all-important. The tragedies we experience become all the more overwhelming. To appreciate the dimension of eternity does not diminish the pain we feel when we suffer but it does enable us to reflect on, and to come to terms with, the fact of suffering in a way that is less desperate, less hopeless.

When my eldest daughter was very young I had to take her to the dentist to have some teeth extracted. The first time this happened she didn't know what was happening. Although anxious at the strange surroundings of the surgery she held on to me tightly, and quickly succumbed to the anaesthetic and fell asleep in my arms.

The second time we went for the same treatment it was very different. She sensed immediately what was to happen and held on to me in the forlorn hope that I would protect her.

> In light of heaven, the worst suffering on earth, a life full of the most atrocious tortures on earth, will be seen to be no more serious than one night in an inconvenient hotel.
>
> *Mother Teresa*

Death – the door to eternity

Christ has turned all our sunsets into dawn.

ST CLEMENT OF ALEXANDRIA

Is death the last sleep? No – it is the last and final awakening.

SIR WALTER SCOTT

I thank my God for graciously granting me the opportunity... of learning that death is the key which unlocks the door to our true happiness.

WOLFGANG AMADEUS MOZART

To the well-organized mind, death is but the next great adventure.

J. K. ROWLING

Death opens unknown doors.

JOHN MASEFIELD

Has this world been so kind to you that you should leave with regret? There are better things ahead than any we leave behind.

C. S. LEWIS

And death shall be no more, Death thou shalt die.

JOHN DONNE

I am the resurrection and the life. He who believes in me will live, even though he dies; and whoever lives and believes in me will never die.

JOHN 11:25–26

The anaesthetist gave the injection in her arm but such was her determination that she remained fully conscious. In the end I had to lie on the operating table by her side holding the gas-mask over her face while she struggled until she subsided into sleep. It was one of the most awful moments of my life. Part of me wanted to lash out at the dentist, grab my little girl and rush out of the operating theatre. Another part of me recognized that this moment of suffering and pain had to be seen against the backdrop of my daughter's whole life and welfare.

And because in the end that is how I chose to see it, I came to accept these awful events. It was the broader view that enabled me to come to terms with present suffering.

In a similar way the Bible encourages us to take a broader view and to see the immediate in the light of the eternal. The pain of the suffering is in no way diminished. But there are the beginnings of a new attitude that enables us to move forward through the suffering.

American Midwest. Lightning and dark clouds over a prairie foretell a possible tornado.

CHAPTER SEVEN

The mystery of healing

Healing is a mystery. It happens naturally and supernaturally. But not everybody is healed. Why some people get healed and others don't is a mystery even to the medical profession. It's the search for healing that often sends those suffering illness in the direction of God.

When Jesus healed

A Jamaican minister prays for a sick child, asking God to heal her..

People live longer today than they ever have before. There is access to very good health care in privileged parts of the world. But instead of satisfying the longing to be healthy,

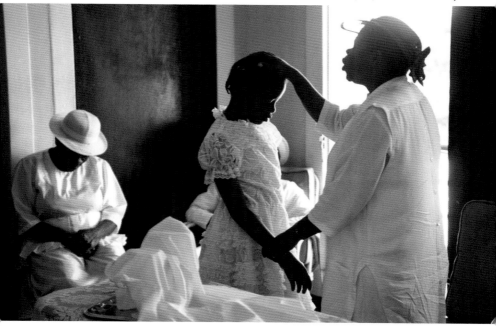

modern advances in medicine simply increase expectations. If the doctors tell us there is no cure for our particular disease then we feel cheated and let down.

When conventional medicine offers no help, people turn with increasing interest to alternative medicines. Diet, relaxation, meditation and homeopathy are all part of the new prescription. There's no doubt that many derive considerable benefit from these alternative therapies which are viewed increasingly by medical practitioners as complementary to conventional medicines.

There's a new interest too in spirituality as an important dimension to personal well-being. Conventional religion may no longer appeal to swathes of the population but books, articles and courses that allow people to explore their inner self are in great demand. There's an idea that if only you can find that secret key that opens the door to inner happiness then you'll be a better person, partner, parent, leader, business manager or whatever your ambition is. People pay good money chasing these therapies in the hope that this so-called holistic approach to life will bring them health, wealth and happiness.

In this climate of finding new paths to healing there's been a rediscovery in the church of Christian teaching about health. More and more churches offer services where the leaders lay hands on those who are unwell and pray for their healing. Stories about Jesus healing people are read from the Bible, and others talk about their experience of healing through prayer. This leads many people who are suffering to come to the church. They may have little or no faith but out of desperation will swallow all their previous objections and ask to be prayed for. Some begin to experience some remission of the symptoms, some find their faith grows, some find that nothing changes, some become disillusioned. It's important to consider what we should expect when in the midst of our suffering we come to church for spiritual help and healing. There's no doubt that Jesus healed people. He had the power to heal those with leprosy, the blind, the deaf and the paralyzed, and even to raise people from the dead. Even more than that, he gave his original disciples the authority to go and do the same: '... to drive out evil spirits and to heal every disease and sickness'. This has led a number of Christians today to claim that God gives us the power to do exactly what Jesus and his first disciples did. Their confidence in God's ability to heal supernaturally today is based on a number of points:

- God loves the world and hates to see people suffer

- God wants everyone to be well, to find wholeness in mind, body and spirit

- God wants people to be aware of his power over evil

- Jesus is the same today as he was when he was on earth healing people

- Jesus promised his power to heal to all those who followed him

- If we have enough faith in God then even the impossible is possible.

In the letter of James, this question of healing is addressed: 'Is any one of you sick? He should call the elders of the church to pray over him and anoint him with oil in the name of the Lord. And the prayer offered in faith will make the sick person well; the Lord will raise him up. If he has sinned, he will be forgiven. Therefore confess your sins to each other and pray for each other so that you may be healed. The prayer of a righteous person is powerful and effective' (James 5:14–16).

The stories about Jesus healing people are for some a great spur to faith. Sick people read them and step by step

Jesus cured many who had diseases, sicknesses and evil spirits, and gave sight to many who were blind. So he replied to the messengers, 'Go back and report to John what you have seen and heard: The blind receive sight, the lame walk, those who have leprosy are cured, the deaf hear, the dead are raised, and the good news is preached to the poor.'

Luke 7:21–22

imagine themselves in the shoes of those who came to Jesus and felt his touch. In their imaginations they open themselves up to the Spirit of the risen Jesus Christ and ask him to fill their lives with his healing power. Such an exercise often provides a sufferer with an experience of inner peace. Some will discover a relief of the symptoms. A few find that they have been healed.

Obviously when a person is suffering and desperate they

Many disabled people come to Lourdes in France, hoping to be healed.

Four incidents when Jesus healed

As Jesus and his disciples, together with a large crowd, were leaving the city, a blind man, Bartimaeus (that is, the Son of Timaeus), was sitting by the roadside begging. When he heard that it was Jesus of Nazareth, he began to shout 'Jesus, Son of David, have mercy on me!'

Many rebuked him and told him to be quiet but he shouted all the more, 'Son of David, have mercy on me!'

Jesus stopped and said, 'Call him.' So they called to the blind man, 'Cheer up! On your feet! He's calling you.' Throwing his cloak aside, he jumped to his feet and came to Jesus.

'What do you want me to do for you?' Jesus asked him. The blind man said, 'Rabbi, I want to see.' 'Go,' said Jesus, 'your faith has healed you.' Immediately he received his sight and followed Jesus along the road.

MARK 10:46–52

A man with leprosy came and knelt before him and said, 'Lord, if you are willing, you can make me clean.'

Jesus reached out his hand and touched the man. 'I am willing' he said. 'Be clean!' Immediately he was cured of his leprosy. Then Jesus said to him, 'See that you don't tell anyone. But go, show yourself to the priest and offer the gift Moses commanded, as a testimony to them.'

MATTHEW 8:2–4

will clutch at any straw. They are in a vulnerable state and therefore come to the church for help with high expectations, especially if they've been encouraged to come forward by someone who's found prayer for healing helpful. It's very important to understand what Jesus was doing and saying when he healed people during his life on earth.

All the healings of Jesus were only temporary remissions. The people he healed and raised from the dead didn't live

Some time later, Jesus went up to Jerusalem for a feast of the Jews. Now there is in Jerusalem near the Sheep Gate a pool, which in Aramaic is called Bethesda and which is surrounded by five covered colonnades. Here a great number of disabled people used to lie – the blind, the lame, the paralyzed. One who was there had been an invalid for thirty-eight years. When Jesus saw him lying there and learned that he had been in this condition for a long time, he asked him, 'Do you want to get well?'

'Sir' the invalid replied, 'I have no-one to help me into the pool when the water is stirred. While I am trying to get in, someone else goes down ahead of me.'

Then Jesus said to him, 'Get up! Pick up your mat and walk.' At once the man was cured; he picked up his mat and walked.

JOHN 5:1–9

Soon afterwards, Jesus went to a town called Nain, and his disciples and a large crowd went along with him. As he approached the town gate, a dead person was being carried out – the only son of his mother, and she was a widow. And a large crowd from the town was with her.

When the Lord saw her, his heart went out to her and he said, 'Don't cry.'

Then he went up and touched the coffin, and those carrying it stood still. He said, 'Young man, I say to you, get up!' The dead man sat up and began to talk, and Jesus gave him back to his mother.

They were all filled with awe and praised God. 'A great prophet has appeared among us,' they said. 'God has come to help his people.'

LUKE 7:11–16

forever – they later died. This wasn't a failure on the part of Jesus. In healing people he wasn't saying that no one should ever fall ill and die.

If we were living in the New Testament times of Jesus, most people would be dead by the time they were fifty. Life expectancy in the West today is almost twice as great as it was in the time of Jesus.

This is due to tremendous advances in medical science,

especially in the last fifty years. Modern health care would seem miraculous to anybody from first-century Palestine. Severed limbs are surgically joined to the body, babies born prematurely survive, hearts and lungs are transplanted, and the majority of people live to their seventies and eighties. All these things are taken for granted in some parts of the world. Christians believe that the human ingenuity responsible for these miraculous advances is God-given and God-inspired. They are as much acts of God as the healings performed supernaturally by Jesus' disciples.

Although Jesus healed very many people he did not heal everybody. When he healed a paralyzed man by the Pool of Siloam, there were many other sick and disabled people there he ignored.

The dramatic healings of Jesus had a very specific purpose. They were to let people know two things: firstly, that a new age was dawning with the coming of the kingdom of God, and secondly, that Jesus was the Son of God.

The hands of the king are the hands of a healer, and so shall the rightful king be known.

J. R. R. Tolkien

When Jesus healed he was putting down markers for his new kingdom. In effect he was saying, 'You think that disease and death are the last word on human life. But I have news for you. God is bringing about a new world from which disease and death will be banished for ever.' To demonstrate the point he healed people and even raised some from the dead.

The new world that God is to bring about has yet to be fully and finally established. Meanwhile, death and disease still hold sway. But, as in the life of Jesus, there will be times today when God breaks into the present order of things to display his power over evil and suffering. It reminds us that a new world is around the corner where there will be 'no more death or mourning or crying or pain'. That is why even today, in spite of the great advances in medical knowledge, there will still be occasional miracles that defy the experts.

How does God answer our prayers?

When we pray to God we can seldom be sure of the outcome. God sees everything whereas we see only a small part. Even though we may be clear what we want God to do, we have to recognize that God sees the whole picture and that we may well be blind to other things that are important.

Jesus taught us to pray to God, 'Your will be done.' This is at the heart of the Lord's Prayer and was echoed by Jesus as he sought to escape the cruel death of crucifixion.

In this way he taught us a new relationship to supernatural power. Those people who practice the occult arts seek to manipulate spiritual power through rituals and spells. Such manipulation is foreign to Jesus' thinking.

Christians cannot command and manipulate the power of God, however worthy the cause. Instead they are called to submit to the sovereign power of God who answers prayers as he decides. His will is supreme.

Sometimes God answers our prayers for healing through the help of doctors, surgery and medicine. These are all part of the world God has made. Even though the doctors and nurses may not recognize God as the source of everything that is good, he nevertheless works through them to help people. In the time of Jesus it was recognized that certain oils had healing properties, and they were rubbed into the body as medicine.

After Jesus had died and left the physical world, his followers met together to pray. When anybody was in trouble or sick the leaders would gather round and pray for the person who was unwell. They were told to anoint the

The Lord's Prayer

Our Father in heaven,
hallowed be your name,
your kingdom come,
your will be done,
on earth as in heaven.
Give us today our daily bread.
Forgive us our sins
as we forgive those who sin
   against us.
Lead us not into temptation
but deliver us from evil.
For the kingdom, the power,
and the glory are yours
now and for ever.

Amen.

sick with oil in the name of the Lord. In other words, they were to administer medicine and pray at the same time. The way to get well was through medication and prayer.

I know someone who suffered from a very serious and rare form of cancer. The prognosis was very bleak. At that time 95 per cent of all people diagnosed with this strain of cancer died within a year.

I went with him to someone who laid hands on his body, in particular where the cancerous growth was. The man prayed that God the Holy Spirit would work through the chemotherapy and radiotherapy to remove the cancer.

As my friend underwent treatment we continued to pray that God would use the treatment to bring healing. The sessions of chemotherapy were very debilitating but, as the X-rays showed, the prayers for healing were answered. The cancer disappeared – nearly twenty years on he is still alive.

What impressed me about the doctors at the hospital was their recognition that the spiritual support that we were offering to our friend through our prayers was just as important as the medical treatment that they were prescribing. They could see that at the very least the prayers were proving to be a great psychological benefit to their patient.

A positive mental and spiritual outlook is a vital part of the healing process in the body. The way we are and the way we think affects our bodies. A person who knows that others are praying for them will find consolation and peace of mind in these prayers. And that peace in their mind sets the tone for their whole body.

If at this moment you try conjuring up images of fresh lemons being cut and squeezed, it is quite likely that your mouth will start watering. These mental images spur your saliva glands into overdrive. It shows the power of the imagination to affect the body.

Our minds, spirits and bodies may have separate words to

describe them but in reality they cannot be held apart. What happens in one dimension of our personality affects the others. So when we begin to pray for healing and open our spirits to God it is not surprising that a spiritual sense of well-being should begin to affect our bodies as we receive medical treatment. This is one way in which God answers our prayers for healing.

Sometimes, in spite of medical advances, doctors are unable to help. Today there seem to be a lot of viruses that seriously affect people, threatening their lives and mystifying the doctors. In her book *Unexpected Healing*, Jennifer Rees Larcombe has described how she was struck down by a mystery virus that left her unable to walk and in a wheelchair. She received expert advice from the medical profession who were unable to prescribe a cure.

After years of illness, which she had come to terms with, Jennifer was speaking in a church. A young woman, who had only recently put her trust in Christ, prayed that Jennifer would be healed by God. And she was. Hers is an extraordinary story. It serves as an example that although God works through medicine he is also free to work beyond it. When doctors can offer no further help it may well be right to ask God to work supernaturally and give the healing which is beyond human understanding to provide.

Jennifer's story is very similar to that of a woman who came to Jesus. For twelve years she had suffered from a haemorrhage. She had spent everything on getting medical help but grew steadily worse. She heard about Jesus and his power to heal and sought him out.

When Jesus was in a large crowd she went up behind him and touched his cloak, as she was convinced that this would be enough to cure her. Her bleeding stopped immediately, and she knew that she was healed.

Even though there was a huge crowd pressing against him, Jesus knew that someone had touched him as he felt

God be in
my head
and in my
understanding;
God be in
my eyes and
in my looking;
God be in
my mouth
and in my
speaking;
God be in my
heart and in
my thinking;
God be at
my end and at
my departing.

*Sarum Primer
Prayer*

the power going out of him. The woman confessed to him what she had done. Jesus told her to be free from her suffering, 'Daughter, your faith has healed you. Go in peace' (Luke 8:48).

These miraculous examples are only some of the ways in which God answers prayer. Sometimes miracles, although prayed for and sought with tears, are notable by their absence. God hears the prayers but chooses to answer in a different way. This can be very difficult to accept, especially when we hear stories of other people being healed. We begin to doubt ourselves. Perhaps God is punishing us. Perhaps he is withholding healing because we have not shown enough faith.

None of these doubts holds up to scrutiny. As we've seen elsewhere in this book, Jesus made it clear that suffering is never a punishment that God inflicts on us. And as for faith, all that God looks for is an openness to him and a willingness to lean on him.

My experience of suffering, and of being with those who suffer, is that when we get to the point where all our emotional and physical energy is drained we are only too ready to cast ourselves on God and implore him to help. That is faith. It is the openness to God that allows him to draw near to us.

He promises always to do this. But not always to heal us this side of the grave. Instead of healing he may bring gifts of strength, peace, gentleness. And the grace to endure.

It is a paradox of life that some of the best people we ever meet are those who have suffered a great deal. Their lives are like still waters that run very deep. There's a quality of inner goodness that has been wrought through all the pain. Conversely, some of the least attractive people are those who are brash and untouched by failure. They seem superficial by comparison with those who have been schooled in the hardship of life's sufferings.

'My grace is sufficient for you, for my power is made perfect in weakness.'

2 Corinthians 12:9

God is burning out of you everything which is unlike himself.

Mother Teresa

I think of a man crippled for years with Parkinson's Disease. I don't even know if he ever prayed for healing. He and his family have known many sadnesses. But to describe his stooped demeanour as radiant would actually be an understatement. His face shines with goodness, and to be with him is as exhilarating as those early days of spring when budding crocuses and daffodils herald the end of dark winter. He does not boast about his faith yet there is an openness to God that nourishes every part of him. That openness has not become a channel of physical healing but it certainly is a means of flooding his whole personality with the love and laughter of God. God has given him the power to endure his sufferings.

Evaristo Tinka (19) from Katabola Angola is fed intravaneously with glucose at a Medicines San Frontiers emergency hospital. Angola's brutal 26-year civil war has displaced around two million people – about a sixth of the population – and 200 die each day according to United Nations estimates.

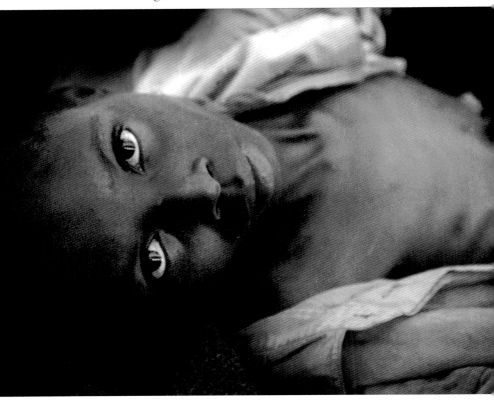

There are times when the refusal of God to heal us physically means that death will come very quickly. Initially that may seem to us to be a failure of our prayers. But to think that way loses sight of the plan of God that the Bible makes so clear.

Death is a reality. It comes to us all. These are truisms, of course. Yet they need to be stated because of the conspiracy of silence that shrouds death in our culture. Dying is part of the natural rhythm of life.

The resurrection of Jesus gives us a new and unique perspective on death. It is not the end of the road but a staging post along the way. For a Christian, what lies beyond the grave is a paradise of great promise where disease and death are banished and crying and grief are no more.

To the Christian who follows Jesus through death into heaven, dying is seen as the ultimate healing. That is why to pray to God for healing from a terminal disease and not to be healed physically is as much an answer to prayer as to be given more life on earth.

The greatest gift that the risen Jesus Christ offers to our death-dreading world is not the secret of getting well but of dying well, in the sure and certain hope of the resurrection to eternal life. Jesus is unique among the great religious leaders, for he alone opened up the way for us all to pass from the land of the dying to the world of the truly alive.

The valley of death's shadow

The Lord is my shepherd, I shall not
  be in want.
He makes me lie down in green
  pastures,
he leads me beside quiet waters,
  he restores my soul.
He guides me in paths of
  righteousness
  for his name's sake.
Even though I walk
  through the valley of the shadow
    of death,
I will fear no evil,
  for you are with me;
your rod and your staff,
  they comfort me.

You prepare a table before me
  in the presence of my enemies.
You anoint my head with oil;
  my cup overflows.
Surely goodness and love will follow me
  all the days of my life,
and I will dwell in the house of the Lord
  for ever.

PSALM 23

The people of New York mark the third anniversary of the 9/11 terrorist attacks.

Jesus said, 'I am the resurrection and the life. Anyone who believes in me will live, even though they die; and whoever lives and believes in me will never die' (John 11:25–26).

How Jesus faced suffering

There is no record of Jesus ever being ill but he experienced a brutal death as cruel as any physical disease. As he faced up to what was to happen to him he prayed: 'Now my heart is troubled, and what shall I say? "Father, save me from this hour?" No, it was for this very reason I came. Father, glorify your name' (John 12:27–28).

For Jesus there were two possible outcomes to his prayer. The first was that he would be rescued and saved from having to go through with being betrayed and crucified. The second was that in surrendering himself to God, others would see the greatness of God in him. Jesus chose the second, and gave all his followers an example of how to encounter suffering.

Our instinctive and natural reaction to all suffering is to escape as quickly as possible. There's nothing dishonourable in that. It's the way we survive as a race. But the person who has begun to centre their life on God has started to live life with a different attitude.

Instead of always seeing themselves at the centre of every situation, Christians try to see everything with God at the centre. The question to learn to ask (it does not come naturally) is, how can God's glory shine through this situation? Looking at difficult circumstances, how can we see the greatness of God?

It was that example of Jesus that the apostle Paul took as his own model as he faced opposition and experienced terrific suffering. 'If I must boast, I will boast of the things that show my weakness. The God and Father of the Lord Jesus, who is to be praised for ever, knows that I am not lying' (2 Corinthians 11:30–31).

CHAPTER EIGHT

A way to God

Books about suffering are seldom of help to those who are actually suffering. The effort of applying yourself to a book is too much to cope with. What follows is simply a personal experience of going through an illness. It is a brief reflection shared in the hope that in the darkness others may find the light of God's presence, which is with those who suffer.

Lord, hear my prayer

Two weeks after having my appendix out I was rushed back into hospital with a pulmonary embolism. I was thirty-six and my wife was expecting our second child. At the time I had no idea how life-threatening a clot on the lung was. All that I knew was that the excruciating pain in my chest and shoulder made it difficult for me to breathe.

After the X-rays I was wheeled back to the ward and then I collapsed by the side of the bed. As doctors and nurses began to rush towards me, quickly pulling the curtains around my bed, I knew that all was not well.

They gave me an injection – the like of which I had never had before – which dulled the pain almost immediately. I was fitted with a drip of heparin to thin the blood, and so began a period of three months when I sank lower than at any other time in my life. All sorts of fears overwhelmed me. Were the doctors telling me the truth? Was I dying? How would Sarah, my wife, cope? What was God doing to me?

I had been a clergyman for eighteen months, during which time I had visited many people in hospital and at home who were sick. This was the first time that I had ever been on the other side of the blanket. But it was to be out of this experience that I began to explore ways of drawing close to God.

Suffering, in any of its forms, saps all your energy. It's difficult to concentrate. The mind wanders all over the place. If there is one thing that the mind keeps coming back to, it's the self. Consequently it's almost impossible to pray for any length of time. However hard I tried to focus my thoughts on God I found that they were always homing themselves back in on myself. So I decided that instead of resisting this and reproaching myself for not being able to think of God, I would run with the direction

my thoughts were going in. I would begin with myself.

Because the embolism was in the lung I was always very conscious of my breathing. Was it shallow? Was it painful? Was it getting worse or better? The twinges of pain that I felt – were they in the lungs or in the muscle? So I started to turn my breathing into praying. Instead of trying to blot out of my mind all my concern about my breathing I deliberately made it the starting point of my prayers.

First, I concentrated on breathing out. I got myself comfortable in bed and consciously breathed in a regular pattern. As I breathed out on a count of four I imagined myself blowing out from my body all the germs and diseases that injured my health. I did this over and over again until I felt that I had expelled everything that I could think of.

I then concentrated on breathing in and imagined with each intake of breath that I was inhaling all the good things that come from God, such as peace, goodness, love, joy, strength. Each time I seemed to breathe more deeply. It felt like breathing in cool mountain air although in reality it was the same disinfectant-perfumed air that fills every hospital ward!

I then remembered that Jesus, after his resurrection, had breathed over his disciples saying, 'Peace be with you' and 'Receive the Holy Spirit.' I imagined Jesus breathing over me and as I breathed in with that thought I sensed myself actually breathing the breath of Jesus.

I then breathed in the peace that he promised, remembering that the word peace in Hebrew, *shalom*, carries with it the idea of healing and wholeness.

And then I consciously inhaled the Holy Spirit who is the very breath of God himself. Peace, the breath of Jesus, the Holy Spirit. The remarkable discovery that I made was that my body gave me a focus and a rhythm for prayer. I drew near to God and had a clear sense that he was drawing near to me, surrounding me with his love.

There are other ways of letting the body be our teacher in prayer. I have always been very queasy about anything to do with blood so have never used this particular method. But I have seen and known others use it to great effect.

Find your pulse, and follow its rhythm as you whisper, 'Jesus, Jesus'. I remember watching a friend, who was dying of cancer, constantly use this prayer when she drew near to her time of healing, as she crossed over to be with God. My abiding memory of the room where she lived and died is a place full of light.

Free me from my anguish

To you, O Lord, I lift up my soul;
in you I trust, O my God.
Do not let me be put to shame,
nor let my enemies triumph over me.
No-one whose hope is in you
will ever be put to shame,
but they will be put to shame
who are treacherous without excuse.

Show me your ways, O Lord,
Teach me your paths;
guide me in your truth and teach me,
for you are God my Saviour,
and my hope is in you all day long.
Remember, O Lord, your great mercy and love,
for they are from of old.
Remember not the sins of my youth
and my rebellious ways;
according to your love remember me,
for you are good, O Lord.

Good and upright is the Lord;
therefore he instructs sinners in his ways.
He guides the humble in what is right
and teaches them his way.
All the ways of the Lord are loving and faithful
for those who keep the demands of his covenant.
For the sake of your name, O Lord,
forgive my iniquity, though it is great.

Just one word is sufficient to make a prayer. The shortest prayer in the New Testament is simply 'Abba'. It means 'Dear Father'. It conjures up a picture of God as a good father who loves his children more than they can ever imagine. The Lord's Prayer which starts with 'Our Father' reveals God the Father as the one who forgives, who provides and who protects. This prayer can be shortened into three short sentences and repeated often: 'Father forgive; Father provide; Father protect.'

The Gospels are full of stories of people who were

Who, then, is the man that fears the Lord?
  He will instruct him in the way chosen for him.
He will spend his days in prosperity,
  and his descendants will inherit the land.
The Lord confides in those who fear him;
  he makes his covenant known to them.
My eyes are ever on the Lord,
  for only he will release my feet from the snare.

Turn to me and be gracious to me,
  for I am lonely and afflicted.
The troubles of my heart have multiplied;
  free me from my anguish.
Look upon my affliction and my distress
  and take away all my sins.
See how my enemies have increased
  and how fiercely they hate me!
Guard my life and rescue me;
  let me not be put to shame,
  for I take refuge in you.
May integrity and uprightness protect me,
  because my hope is in you.

Redeem Israel, O God,
  from all their troubles!

PSALM 25

suffering and came to Jesus. And one way of becoming aware of his presence is to see yourself in the shoes of those who came to him. The one I used most often, especially when I was in bed on an intravenous drip, was the story of the woman who had been haemorrhaging for twelve years.

I would hold onto the sheet and imagine that I was holding on to the tunic of Jesus. In my head, or quietly aloud, I would whisper, 'Jesus, Son of God, have mercy on me, Jesus, Son of God, have mercy on me, Jesus, Son of

Taste and see that the Lord is good

I will extol the Lord at all times;
  his praise will always be on my lips.
My soul will boast in the Lord;
  let the afflicted hear and rejoice.
Glorify the Lord with me:
  let us exalt his name together.

I sought the Lord, and he answered me;
  he delivered me from all my fears.
Those who look to him are radiant;
  their faces are never covered with shame.
This poor man called, and the Lord heard him;
  he saved him out of all his troubles.
The angel of the Lord encamps around those who fear him,
  and he delivers them.

Taste and see that the Lord is good;
  blessed is the man who takes refuge in him.
Fear the Lord, you his saints,
  for those who fear him lack nothing.
The lions may grow weak and hungry,
  but those who seek the Lord lack no good thing.

Come, my children, listen to me;
  I will teach you the fear of the Lord.
Whoever of you loves life
  and desires to see many good days,

God, have mercy on me.' The feel of the sheet between my fingers became a tangible reminder of the presence of Jesus.

When I tired of praying further I would end by recalling the words Jesus spoke to the woman who held on to him. 'Your faith has made you well.'

When I had more strength and could concentrate more I found that the psalms in the Bible often gave me the words I wanted to pray. Two in particular stood out. These psalms are full of praise that God is with the broken-hearted and the crushed in spirit.

keep your tongue from evil
and your lips from speaking lies.
Turn from evil and do good;
seek peace and pursue it.

The eyes of the Lord are on the righteous,
and his ears are attentive to their cry;
the face of the Lord is against those who do evil,
to cut off the memory of them from the earth.

The righteous cry out, and the Lord hears them;
he delivers them from all their troubles.
The Lord is close to the broken-hearted
and saves those who are crushed in spirit.

A righteous man may have many troubles,
but the Lord delivers him from them all;
he protects all his bones,
not one of them will be broken.

Evil will slay the wicked;
the foes of the righteous will be condemned.
The Lord redeems his servants;
no-one will be condemned who takes refuge in him.

PSALM 34

All shall be well

Sometimes what we are suffering makes us inactive in some way, which is very frustrating. Not having anything to do makes us feel so useless and worthless. We're for ever apologizing for being such a nuisance and a bother to others. We feel that we're not pulling our weight and that we're a burden.

In our society a person's worth is often measured by what they do and what they achieve. The opening question in most conversations is, 'So what do you do?' If you're unemployed, redundant, sick, retired, or off work through illness that question can make you feel very defensive.

Our achievement-orientated society makes people who don't or can't do anything feel very small. People who suffer, in addition to the pain they already bear through illness, can begin to feel bad about themselves because they're not doing anything. I certainly felt that.

I was greatly helped by the insight that Jesus himself moved from a period of intense activity to a period of inactivity when he was arrested, bound and crucified. He found himself a victim of other people's plans. Yet it was in this apparently useless and inactive part of his life on the cross that God used him for the salvation of the world.

When we first find ourselves laid up we are following in the footsteps of Jesus every bit as much as when we are busying ourselves with endless things to do. It is not being worthless. Being laid up is being like Christ, available to God.

When we're suffering it's often, although not always, a great comfort to be visited by friends. The best ones never outstay their welcome and see immediately when you need to be alone again. The best ones give to you and do not sap your energy.

When at times I had given up praying I found it helpful when special friends came. I remember them laying their hands on me praying that God would make me well. The heaviness of the presence of their hands on my head and

When pain is to be borne, a little courage helps more than much knowledge, a little human sympathy more than much courage, and the least tincture of the love of God more than all.

C. S. Lewis

shoulders spoke to me of the power of God and the warmth of his love. It was good to feel their physical strength.

Sometimes when I'm visiting someone who's sick I'll not only lay hands on them, but also anoint them with oil. Again the physical sensation can be a sign of the kindness of God, which is ointment to one's soul.

If we could look into a crystal ball, and we saw suffering ahead, all of us would shrink back and choose a different path. Although none of us would ever choose to suffer it is a remarkable fact of life that those who suffer can sometimes look back and even be thankful for some of the things that they have learnt along the way. Things about themselves and things about God. Not always, but sometimes. This adds to the mystery of the existence of suffering in a world fashioned by the God of love. These things are not easily understood. They require faith. The faith that believes that in the end, in the words of Julian of Norwich, 'all shall be well and all shall be well and all manner of thing shall be well'.

It is the faith of Paul, who wrote 'And we know that in all things God works for the good of those who love him' (Romans 8:28). And it's the faith of Jesus Christ, who says to the suffering world: 'I am making everything new.'

A vision of Jesus to Julian of Norwich

And these words: You will not be overcome, were said very insistently and strongly, for certainty and strength against every tribulation which may come. He did not say: You will not be troubled, you will not be belaboured, you will not be disquieted; but he said: You will not be overcome. God wants us to pay attention to these words, and always to be strong in faithful trust, in well-being and in woe, for he loves us and delights in us, and so he wishes us to love him and delight in him and trust greatly in him, and all will be well.

Picture Acknowledgments

p. 6–7 Frank Schwere/Getty Images Ltd

p. 9 BRT PHOTO/Alamy

pp. 10–11 AFP/Getty Images Ltd

p. 12 Paula Bronstein/Getty Images Ltd

pp. 14–15 Tom Stoddart Archive/Getty Images Ltd

p. 17 Getty Images Ltd

pp. 20–21 Digital Vision

p. 24 Mary Evans Picture Library

p. 27 Nicholas Rous/Lion Hudson

p. 31 Paula Bronstein/Stringer/Getty Images Ltd

p. 32–33 2006 Mike Goldwater/Getty Images Ltd

p. 34 Sipa Press/Rex Features

p. 41 © 1992 photo SCALA, Florence – courtesy of the
    Ministero Beni e Att. Culturali

p. 46 Design Pics Inc/Alamy

p. 53 Sandra Baker/Alamy

p. 55 Peter Turnley/Corbis

p. 58 Abid Katib/Getty Images Ltd

p. 62 Mirrorpix

p. 64 Dean Mouhtaropoulos/Getty Images Ltd

p. 67 Per-Anders Pettersson/Getty Images Ltd

p. 68 National Geographic/Getty Images Ltd

p. 71 Getty Images Ltd

p. 75 Andy Rous

p. 79 Richard Cooke/Alamy

p. 82 Wathiq Khuzaie/Stringer/Getty Images Ltd

pp. 84–85 National Geographic/Getty Images Ltd

p. 86 Oliver Benn/Alamy

p. 89 Cristian Baitg reportage/Alamy

p. 97 Ami Vitale/Alamy

p. 99 Stephen Chernin/Getty Images Ltd

p. 100 Andy Rous

p. 102 Various images GmbH & Co. KG/Alamy

p. 109 National Geographic/Getty Images Ltd